EVERY
DREAMER'S
HANDBOOK

WILL PHILLIPS

A STEP-BY-STEP GUIDE
TO UNDERSTANDING
AND BENEFITING
FROM YOUR
DREAMS

Kensington Books

KENSINGTON BOOKS are published by

Kensington Publishing Corp.
850 Third Avenue
New York, NY 10022

Engravings on cover art courtesy of The Bettmann Archive:
Man in the Moon;
Sun's Face, woodcut, 1830:
Alarm Clock, woodcut, 1880:
Drawing of an Eye.

First Kensington Trade Paperback Printing: May, 1996

ISBN 1-57566-048-2

10 9 8 7 6 5 4 3 2 1

Printed in the United States of America

To Maggie, Gabe, and Noah
for your friendship

And to all those
who strive to live in harmony
with the Primordial Thought.

Oceans of feeling
Rise in clouds of vapor dreams
And the rain cleanses.

ACKNOWLEDGMENTS

I would like to express my deepest gratitude to the dream educators who have gone before me blazing trails, and letting people know that they needn't rely on a therapist to benefit from their dreams. Many of you I've had the privilege of getting to know personally; others I feel I've come to know through your writings. Each of you has inspired me by sharing your unique perspective.

My heartfelt thanks to the late Jane Roberts, Ann Faraday, Gayle Delaney, Ken Kelzer, John Sanford, Patricia Garfield, Montegue Ullman, Loma Flowers, Stanley Krippner, Bob Trowbridge, Ann Sayre Wiseman, Stephen LeBerge, and so many others whose work has influenced me. And to my friends, family, students, and readers who have shared their dream lives with me; thank you all for your courage, generosity, and openness.

I would also like to express my sincere appreciation to Evelyn Miller for her invaluable comments and suggestions and to Chris Hudson and Lori Solensten, whose early encouragement gave me the faith to see this project through to completion.

And, of course, my special thanks to Gabe Phillips and Noah Phillips for their terrific illustrations.

CONTENTS

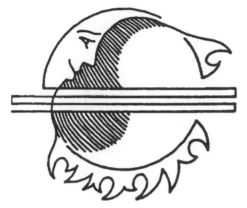 **Introduction**

When in the midst of an overwhelming personal crisis or major life decision, who hasn't sometimes wished for a great sage to ask for guidance? The ancients consulted their oracles, the Celts sought out the Druids, Native Americans and other indigenous tribes went on vision quests and consulted their shamans. Prophets, priestesses, popes, and psychiatrists have all been relied upon for wisdom and counsel. Yet there is an ever-present source of guidance available to everyone that requires no pilgrimage, no ritual, no fasting, penance, or financial sacrifice. With nothing more than courage and honesty, you can access the wisdom of your Greater Being by learning to understand your dreams.

Some people complain, of course, that dream symbols are too bizarre, the plots too confused and the images too plastic to make any sense. Therefore they conclude that their dreams are either meaningless or so complex that only a trained professional or gifted psychic could possibly comprehend them. Unfortunately, that view is often reinforced by both the psychiatric community, with its emphasis on psychoanalytic theories, and by "psychic" dream interpreters who would encourage you to rely on their abilities instead of your own. But take heart; it doesn't have to be that difficult. You already possess all the skills necessary to understand your dreams, and this book will provide clear instructions on how to apply them.

The Guided Interview method is an easily learnable approach I developed while teaching classes in dream understanding and working with thousands of dreams. It centers on a fourteen-item worksheet that offers a personal orientation, flexible structure, proven techniques, and helpful, open-ended questions. It is not an effortless formula nor will it automatically condense your dream into a fortune-cookie message. But its straightforward simplicity has often proven extraordinarily helpful, particularly when a dreamer has no idea where to begin. An added benefit is that the Guided Interview approach doesn't require large blocks of uninterrupted time. Many people have discovered the rewards of dreamwork but still have to deal with the reality of busy schedules. For them, one of the worksheet's most helpful features is its ability to serve as a "mental bookmark" while they mull over a dream throughout the day.

Individuals can use the Guided Interview Worksheet by themselves to further their personal and spiritual growth. Couples can use it to enhance their relationship. Families can use it to strengthen parent-child bonds. For counselors, it can serve as a valuable communication tool to add to their repertoire.

The first three chapters of the book will address the benefits of dream exploration, offer tips for improving your recall, and discuss the results of an informal experiment to determine whether or not dreams are meaningful. In chapters four through seven, the Guided Interview Worksheet is applied to a sample dream so that you can see exactly how each worksheet item helps to reveal aspects of an actual dream.

Real life dreamwork in a variety of settings is the focus of the next two chapters. Transcripts of spontaneous dreamwork as it actually unfolded are presented in chapter eight. These offer a clear picture of how three different individuals each came to an understanding of what their dream was saying to them. Chapter nine explores the benefits of sharing your dreams with others as well as precautions that should be taken before doing so. This chapter also demonstrates how you can use dreams to exercise your creativity, strengthen family bonds, and increase intimacy in your relationships.

Chapters ten through thirteen contain advanced lessons in dreamwork. They describe how you can intentionally dream about anything you wish, have your dreams respond to specific concerns, and even consciously alter your dreams *while you are still asleep*. You also will discover how dreamwork can eliminate or reduce the number of nightmares you may have, and how to benefit from your frightening dreams in the process. Chapter eleven contains examples of dreams that appeared to come true and explores why such dreams occur and how they can be recognized in time to make a difference. Immediately following in chapter twelve is a theoretical explanation of *how* dreams come true. Whether you accept the hypothesis or not, I think you will find the essay challenging and thought-provoking. The final chapter, then, considers individual and planetary wholeness as ultimate goals of dreamwork.

For those of you who seek the support of other dreamers, I urge you to consider a subscription to the Dream Network (P.O. Box 1026, Moab, Utah 84532). Also, the Association for the Study of Dreams (P.O. Box 1600, Vienna, Virginia 22183) is made up of many of the most dedicated and supportive dream educators and researchers in the world. I have found the ASD's annual conferences an invaluable resource and a rare opportunity to meet and learn with a wide array of skilled dreamworkers.

Just as human beings are born with two legs for walking, we also possess both intellect and intuition. While it is possible to get by relying on only one or the other, graceful living requires a balance between the two. Dreamwork helps to create that balance by providing the opportunity to use these two skills in harmony. Through dreamwork our creativity is awakened, our relationships are improved, our hidden tragedies and triumphs are resolved, and we are able to safely rehearse responses to all kinds of situations. I offer the following material as a field guide to the most universal of human experiences. My greatest wish is that it might help to enrich your everyday life with the wisdom of your dreams.

Chapter 1

Why Bother with Dreams?

An Introduction to the Comfort Zone

Ask a scientist to define dreaming. His (or her) explanation is likely to center around the "random" firings of synapses in the brain that are relayed to the cortex, which then tries to weave a story around the resultant images. Then ask that same scientist to describe a kiss. He may reply that it is a slow rotation of the mandible while simultaneously flexing the *orbicularis oris*, possibly including sebum exchange. Even if both definitions are scientifically accurate, they hardly convey the actual experience of either dreaming or kissing.

If you really want to understand dreams, you will need to take a look at some of your own. Like any other endeavor, dreamwork requires an investment of effort in order to realize potential benefits. It is, however, a pretty safe investment. The only thing required of you is a willingness to look at what is going on inside yourself and enough discipline to record whatever portion of a dream you may remember. And maybe a few dollars for a spiral notebook and a dependable flashlight.

So what are the benefits? Will dreamwork increase your income? Improve your social life? Get you a better job? Save your marriage? What, exactly, can you get from learning to understand your dreams that you do not normally get from waking life?

While it's true that dreams contain a wealth of innovative ideas and boundless opportunities to rehearse and replay responses to waking situations, these are all secondary benefits. The primary function of dreamwork is to help bring you to a point of inner balance. This point of balance is hidden within each moment of time as an invisible range of experience. It has always been here, it is here right now as you read these words (and as I write them) and it will always be here. At the center of this range is a profound state of contentment and well-being I call the "Comfort Zone." Since it is essentially a feeling of equilibrium, the Comfort Zone has the odd characteristic of being more noticeable for its absence than for its presence. It's like the temperature of your house. When it's too cold, you notice it. And when it's too hot, you notice it. But when it's just right, you will probably not notice it.

There are those who denounce the Comfort Zone, claiming it leads to boredom and stagnation. But I contend that there is a time to be bored and stagnant. Those feelings create a longing for change. Then, when you have been bored and stagnant long enough, it becomes intolerably uncomfortable. At that point the only way to stay in the Comfort Zone is to take decisive action.

The challenge of remaining centered in the Comfort Zone from moment to moment is like that of a ship's captain staying on course during an ocean crossing. Excessive idleness, for instance, may cause you to feel ill at ease as you drift out of the Comfort Zone in one direction. Yet over-ambition can result in equivalent discomfort as you drift off in the opposite direction. When there is too little human intimacy in your life, you will begin to feel increasingly uncomfortable. On the other hand, too much social contact can be equally disconcerting. To stay on course, a ship's captain depends upon his compass. If he unintentionally veers a few degrees off, a quick glance at his instruments can give him the guidance he needs to determine his position and correct his error. But what compass can dependably and accurately reflect our life position? How can we tell when we have veered a few degrees off course?

Laws and social expectations are among the more immediate forms of guidance in our daily lives. But both are constantly changing and designed more for groups than for individuals. There are also scriptures and other forms of religious guidance. They change less often and are more likely to address personal concerns, but are still externally imposed and subject to hotly debated interpretations. Probably our most commonly used source of guidance is the feedback we get from family and friends. The main problem with this lies in trying to sort out honest feedback from that which has hidden motives. Maybe you are fortunate enough to know someone who will always be absolutely honest with you. Even their perceptions are inevitably going to be distorted by their own biases and limited understanding of your circumstances. And while you might have a more comprehensive understanding of your situation than anyone else, you may not always be willing or able to be entirely honest with even yourself. There is, therefore, a clear need for something that will call us on our pretenses and reveal to us our blind spots. This is where dreams can help.

The Comfort Zone Compass

You need not interpret a dream in order for it to influence the course of your life. Even if you cannot recall the details of what happened, the mood and general feeling of your dream will act as a bridge between your intuitive wisdom and your waking awareness. Sometimes these lingering feelings will inexplicably attract you toward a particular activity. On other occasions they might zap you with a cattle-prod jolt to steer you away from a dangerous course of action. Unless you completely shut out your dreams and steer without a compass, they will continually nudge you back toward the Comfort Zone.

Holding onto the mood of a half-remembered dream results in benefits on an instinctive level. Recalling the details and consciously working with the themes and images, however, can bring this instinctive awareness to a conscious level, thus increasing the benefits. The Guided Interview Worksheet (see Appendix) was created for this purpose. The worksheet, which will be introduced in Chapter 4, follows the natural progression of a remembered dream as closely as possible. By clarifying and amplifying the basic elements of the dream, it helps the dreamer to elicit insights, identify feelings and, most importantly, decide upon an appropriate course of action.

Children are born with an instinctive responsiveness to their dreams which keeps them close to the Comfort Zone. Unfortunately as they grow into adolescence and adulthood they tend to lose touch with their dreams and begin to seek out external forms of guidance. Why does this happen? One reason may be that dreams have not traditionally been valued by the adults who are most important to them. Another might be that children quickly learn that social acceptance often requires a denial of spontaneous feelings. Since dreams are feeling generators, children may close off to them so as to avoid social censure.

Yet denying our dreams does not stop them from occurring. It only puts us out of touch with the feelings they use to tempt and prod us back toward the Comfort Zone. The further away we get from those feelings, the harder our dreams will work to get us to acknowledge them again. The way they do it, of course, is to create images and situations that are increasingly intense until it is virtually impossible to ignore them.

Consequently, people who rarely remember dreams will generally recall only the most vivid ones. Often these dreams are frightening and the dreamer's reaction is to try even harder to shut them out. But dreams are as resourceful as they are persistent. They will present sce-narios of every kind, from horrifying to ecstatic, until they find an image memorable enough to make it into the dreamer's waking recog-nition. This is the same type of approach used by advertisers. Their only intent is to get you to remember their product. It makes little difference whether the advertisement is memorably beautiful or mem-orably ugly. Their goal is simply to keep you aware of the product so that you will remember and purchase it. Similarly, dreams will often use disgusting or grotesque images to imprint the dream on your mind so that you might instinctively act upon it.

Although all of us may require an occasional jolt from our dreams, there is no need to be continually disturbed by them. Dreams will frighten you only if it takes fear to motivate you to action. As you become more willing to acknowledge the unpleasant dreams, they will begin to evolve into more tolerable varieties. This is particularly true if you make efforts to understand them and act upon their insights. Once you have established a working relationship with your dreams, they can then afford to be more polite.

Naturally it may take more than a bit of courage to invite dreams back into your life after having been long out of touch with them. Dreams are unpredictable; they will shatter your preconceptions and show you things you may never have consciously chosen to look at. Although dreams can never hurt you, they will not hesitate to scare you half to death. Sometimes that is what it takes to bring a long avoided emotional truth to your attention. You can try to shut your dreams out of awareness, but you will never be completely successful. The more tightly you grasp the doorknob, the louder they will bang on the other side. Your efforts would be better spent acknowledging their inevitability, learning to understand their mannerisms, and beginning to establish an alliance with them.

So how do you muster up the courage to take that first step into this dark and mysterious, yet once familiar realm? It usually begins with a basic understanding of the naturalness, purpose, and benefits of dreaming. Too many myths still abound that encourage people to fear their dreams when, in fact, dreams are essential to our emotional well-being. They serve as a common denominator that binds together every race, creed, culture, sex, and age group. It might even be said that dreams are humankind's most Common Sense.

Merely acknowledging the theoretical benefits of dreaming on an intellectual level, however, is not enough. The second step toward reclaiming ownership of your dreams requires that you make a leap of faith and allow a dream to enter your conscious awareness. Specific advice on various methods of recording dreams and improving recall will be presented in the following chapter.

Once you are dealing with an actual dream, rather than with your expectations and conceptualizations, you have reached the third step: Experience. Suddenly, personal dream adventures replace your ideas and assumptions. No longer are you sitting off to the side reading books and listening to other people tell of their experiences. You feel the power of your own dream. You see it, hear it, taste it, even smell it. It is your creation, your most personal possession. Before long, that first dream will lead to another and yet another. Gradually, you will become familiar with your own unique style of dreaming. Your personal dreamscapes will be populated with characters of all types whose intentions, needs, and motivations are known only to you. The fourth and final step of the reclamation process is to establish communication and begin to form alliances with these characters.

It is vital to understand that your dreams alone will no more resolve your problems than a compass alone will steer a ship. The responsibility of your dreams is to reflect dependably and accurately your life position. Your waking responsibility is to attend to your dreams and take steps to ensure that the decisions you make from day to day reflect those dream insights.

As boisterous as they may sometimes be, your dreams will respect dimensional boundaries and remain in their own realm. The only exception is when, by choosing to act upon them, you invite them into your waking life. They will never subject you to anything you are unable to cope with; neither will they stand idly by while you steadily advance toward danger. They will show you where improvements can be made in your life, but will leave it to you to make them.

Even when your dreams are forgotten, they still leave lingering feelings that color and influence your waking life to some extent. By making a minimal investment of time and effort, it is possible to bring these dream memories and insights to full waking awareness. At times you may be shocked by their grotesque imagery. On other occasions they will lift you into ecstasy by giving you the experience of having your every desire fulfilled. Whether they motivate you with fright or delight, they always have a purpose; to nudge you back into the Comfort Zone.

So before deciding that dreams are unworthy of your attention, try attending to your own for awhile. You may find they help you to maintain a sense of balance and self-awareness. And this ability to remain centered in the Comfort Zone will benefit you in every area of your life.

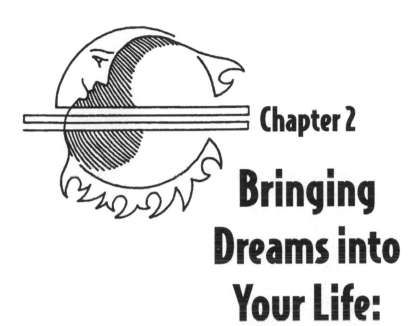

Chapter 2

Bringing Dreams into Your Life:

Suggestions for Improving Recall

More than half the people in a typical first-night dream class complain of having difficulty recalling dreams. Considering the current level of technology, it certainly can't be attributed to a lack of recording options. Besides the traditional spiral notebook and ballpoint pen there are now electronic typewriters, computers, and voice-activated microcassette recorders. You can even videotape an account of your dream. Neither can a shortage of recall techniques be offered as an explanation since there are a number of these available as well. The fact is that despite an abundance of resources, most adults rarely remember their dreams. This leads me to conclude that dream recall is about ninety-eight percent desire and two percent method.

Nevertheless, techniques do sometimes help some people to remember their dreams. For that reason I have put together the following collection of tips and suggestions. Do keep in mind, though, that no technique can guarantee you a dream. The reason is simple: when an individual has a clear understanding of what he or she can expect from dreamwork and is willing to pursue the truth no matter where it leads, elaborate recall and recording techniques are unnecessary. And if even the deepest longing to recall a dream is mingled with a fear of what the dream may reveal, then no technique in existence is likely to be effective.

There are three basic prerequisites for bringing a dream into the world. Every dream recall technique ever devised is essentially a creative combination of these elements:

1) Readiness   (being prepared to record dreams whenever they are remembered)

2) Willingness   (possessing motivation and perseverance)

3) A sense of expectation   (having faith)

My own preference is to record my dream notes on a yellow notepad which I keep on a night table within easy reach of my bed. On top of the pad, I place a quality ballpoint pen and a small, dependable flashlight. I also keep a spare pen in the drawer in case the first one runs dry or rolls off the table and under the bed. Occasionally, when I've been spending a fair amount of time playing musical instruments, I also keep a tape recorder nearby. To date, I've filled about half of a ninety minute cassette tape with original dream melodies.

On the first line of the notepad, just before going to bed, I write the next morning's date and day of the week. This helps to create the sense of expectation that is so important to recalling a dream. Then I jot down a brief predream entry describing highlights of the day's events. My weekly appointment book is a big help here. A glance at the day's notes while making my predream entry enables me to recall the kind of highly charged events, letters, phone calls, health concerns or even movies and TV shows that are likely to generate dream material. Then as I'm falling asleep I sometimes spend a few minutes visualizing something I would like to see manifest in my waking life. Or perhaps I might redream a scene from the previous night (redreaming will be discussed at length in chapter seven).

The state of sleep is not stagnant. It goes through waves. Several times during the night you go from deep sleep to near-wakefulness and back again. If you are strongly motivated and willing to persevere, it is not too difficult to learn to awaken yourself after a dream while the images are still fresh in your mind. When I awaken from a dream during the night, I generally record the time I awakened and jot down a few notes that will remind me of the dream in the morning. This usually takes only five or ten minutes, after which I fall asleep with the comfort of knowing that later I will be able to review the dream more completely. If a dream is particularly vivid, however, I may write it out in detail right then. The problem is that it's not unusual to recall several dreams in a single night. If I were to elaborate on all of them immediately upon awakening, I would spend my days bleary-eyed .

The next morning I use my night notes to prompt me into remembering the dream in its entirety. Then I record the dream in my computer or on a notepad and store it in a 3-ring binder. This allows me later to add thoughts and associations that connect the dream to my waking life.

Whenever possible I try to find the time (or if the dream was especially powerful, MAKE the time) to work with the dream right then. Otherwise, I carry the dream around in the back of my mind and sort of chew on it throughout the day.

Although this is my favorite method, it is not necessarily the right one for you. The "best method" for recalling dreams is simply the one that works best in your own circumstances. I offer the following techniques in hopes that they might prove helpful in breaking the ice and getting the dream river flowing.

1)   Keep your recording materials within easy reach of your bed. Walking even a few steps to your dresser will seem like a super-human task at three o'clock in the morning. Then, even if you do manage to find your paper and pen, there is an excellent chance you will have forgotten the dream.

2)   Review your own personal reasons for wanting to get in touch with your dreams. Write down a specific question you would like your dreams to address.

3)   Record fragments if that is all you get. When attempting to record their first dreams, short vignettes are all that most people remember. Yet I have seen life-changing insights revealed to dreamers who bothered to make note of them.

4)   Dreams are often remembered in reverse order. That is, you initially recall only the final scene. If this should happen, ask yourself what occurred just before that scene. The rest of the dream

may very well come back to you.

5) Try to neither judge nor censor your dreams. Everyone occa-
    sionally dreams of graphic violence and outlandish sexual situa-
    tions.   Dreams are the natural environment for that kind of
    activity. I once had a very respectable and law-abiding elderly
    woman in a dream class whose first reported dream involved a
    police raid on her house for possession of cocaine! Find the
    courage to remember all kinds of dreams, for as long as you
    acknowledge only certain types while ignoring others you will
    be like a traveler who has been given valid directions but refuses
    to make left turns.

6) An earthy but very effective Native American recall technique
    is to drink about eight to twelve ounces of water just before
    going to bed. The gradually increasing pressure on the bladder
    will generally awaken you at the end of a dream cycle. The
    modern (and more intrusive) version is to set an alarm clock to
    go off every two or three hours throughout the night. If you
    decide to try this latter technique, or if you normally awaken to
    an alarm, choose one that will not jar you awake. Train yourself
    to regard the alarm not as an indication to jump out of bed but
    instead as a trigger to remember your dreams.

7) Be willing to write your dreams down. At some point you will
    probably wake up in the middle of the night with a powerful
    dream. You may be tempted not to write it down, feeling cer-
    tain that such a vivid experience could not possibly be forgot-
    ten. Don't count on it. If you don't want to write it out in
    detail, at least jot down a few key words or describe mental
    snapshots of the dream. (Note: be certain you really wrote it
    down and did not just dream that you did. I'm not kidding!
    This will be discussed further in chapter ten.)

8) Examine your attitudes and beliefs. Do you tend to inhibit
    expressions of emotion in your waking life? If so, you may be
    doing the same thing with your dreams. Try cutting loose a lit-
    tle in your waking life when it's not going to do any harm.

Throw a champagne glass into the fireplace. Climb a tree. Take a spontaneous weekend trip. Waste a little something.

9)   If you recall nothing in the morning, lie quietly in bed for awhile. Changing positions will sometimes jog a memory. If you are still unable to remember a dream, just write a line or two about your feelings and mood at the moment. It may bring back a dream, and it will at least get you into the habit of writing down something in the morning.

10) Develop a pre-sleep ritual, whether it involves visualization, prayer, meditation, or some other means of turning your attention inward.

11) Children and visually-oriented adults often prefer to diagram their dreams or combine drawings with cartoon balloons instead of writing out the entire account.

12) Napping or altering your sleep patterns sometimes helps to stimulate recall. Sleeping alone in a special place may have a similar effect. Do make certain that you are getting adequate rest.

13) Some people choose to record their dreams on tape rather than on paper. The main advantage of tape recording is that it takes less effort during the night (in fact, I once awakened with a dream on tape that I had no memory of dictating). Also, the voice inflections sometimes carry meaning that is missed on paper. Unfortunately, the same other-worldly narration which is so fascinating to hear may also be very difficult to understand. And the time you save during the night is spent the next morning when you go to transcribe the recording into your journal. Additional problems with tape recording dreams arise if you sleep with a partner. Aside from the concern of waking them up with the sound of your voice, there is a danger of unintentional self-censorship. It is quite possible that those embarrassing details which you neglect to mention may be the key to understanding the dream.

14) When you discover the intricate connections that link even a

single dream to your waking life, you will have tapped into the greatest motivator of all. After receiving the treasures hidden within your first few dreams, it is unlikely that you will ever again casually dismiss them.

15) Most people who complain of never remembering their dreams have, for whatever reasons, never really made a consistent effort to record them. Keeping and reviewing a written record of your dreams virtually guarantees that more will come.

16) Be gentle with yourself. Despite your best efforts, there will be times when you come up empty-handed. If the message is of particular importance, it will call again.

Sometimes it seems that recalling a dream is like trying to raise the Titanic. Most people feel this way at first. But if your desire is strong and you are willing to face your fear of the unknown, it is possible to float a dream up from these oceanic depths to the surface where it can be viewed in the full light of consciousness. If you go no further, however, the dream will gradually sink back into the depths to be forgotten. Writing the dream down is like attaching outriggers that enable it to remain at the surface indefinitely. There its secrets can be revealed and its value more fully appreciated and utilized.

It makes no difference how long it has been since you last remembered a dream. Nor does it matter whether you have access to all of the latest technical innovations. If you are ready, willing and have developed a sense of expectation, you will soon have an abundance of dream material.

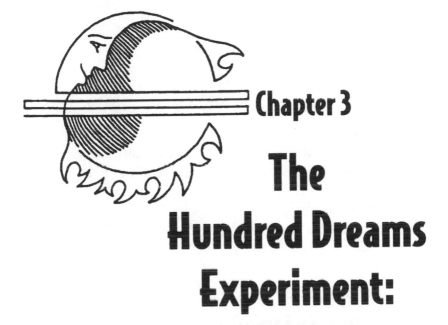

Chapter 3

The Hundred Dreams Experiment:

How Many Have Meaning?

The debate as to whether dreams are meaningful has undoubtedly gone on since the first human grunted out a dream. In all likelihood, the various positions that were pondered around the fire back then were probably not very different from those being discussed in university research facilities even now. At one end of the scale are those who maintain that dreams are the meaningless meanderings of an off-duty brain. Diametrically opposed to that viewpoint are those who contend that all dreams have symbolic significance, regardless of length or environmental factors during sleep. Of course, there are always the "middle-of-the-roaders" who hedge their bets by claiming that some dreams are meaningful and others are not.

Oddly enough, it has always been that last category that has bothered me the most. Admittedly, I would prefer to think that dreams embody some form of cryptic inner wisdom. Yet if presented with overwhelming evidence to the contrary, I could live quite comfortably with the idea that after spending all day engaged in worldly survival and orchestrating countless bodily functions, our brains simply need to take the night off. But the prospect of judging certain dreams to be meaningful and casting others out as nonsense strikes me as incredibly arrogant. It seems akin to claiming that everything in creation has a purpose except mosquitoes, tonsils, and poison ivy. Just because I can't see their reason for being, does that mean there is none?

By the time I had collected approximately a thousand dreams, the question of meaningfulness became increasingly significant. About two hundred of my dream journal entries were transparent enough for me to easily recognize definite, meaningful connections to my daily activities. However, the remaining eight hundred or so that I had given up on after a cursory glance remained complete mysteries. It suddenly occurred to me that if only twenty percent of my dreams had any relevance to my waking life, then eighty percent of the time I spent writing them down was wasted. It was at that point I made a decision. I would examine the next one hundred consecutive dreams to be recorded in my journals and see how many could be identified as directly reflecting the current concerns of my life in a meaningful way.

In an effort to make it easier to recognize any possible connections between my dreams and waking life, I began habitually writing a brief summary of the day's events before going to sleep. This was the origin of the predream entry that has continued to be enormously helpful. I disciplined myself to write down every recalled dream, whether it occurred during the night or in the morning. On a few occasions, some seemingly insignificant event from my workday would trigger a dream memory from the previous night. Those, too, I recorded and set about scrutinizing for meaning, applying suggestions from every dream book I could lay my hands on. It took just under four months to compile the hundred dreams. Some were pages long while others were only one or two sentence fragments. But I treated every dream with equal respect, as if it had significance, though it may have appeared nonsensical at first glance.

Each dream was reviewed as soon as possible while its waking life context was still relevant and accessible. At first, my approach to analyzing them consisted largely of identifying the most outstanding events, characters, and images, then free-associating with them. Although many relevant insights came to light, a sense of dissatisfaction and emptiness began to creep in after several weeks of approaching my dreams from this perspective. I was haunted by the suspicion that my method was somehow neglecting an entire dimension of dreaming. It was as if I were studying rare and beautiful birds by capturing, dissecting, and microscopically examining them.

Around that time, I slipped into a period of emotional doldrums that seemed to cling no matter what I did to try to shake them off.

After many melancholy days, I awakened one morning filled to over-flowing with an inexplicable lighthearted joyousness. As I laid in bed savoring the feelings, dream images began to resurface. I remembered. being with a close friend from high school who shared my birth date. Although we had lost touch in waking life many years before, in my dream she and I had been hang-gliding side by side over the Rocky Mountains. The feelings of deep friendship, acceptance, and freedom that surrounded me in the dream remained after I awakened and stayed with me throughout the day.

I recorded the dream in detail in my journal, but it would have felt like a travesty to pluck out images and free-associate with them. All I wanted was to bask in the warmth of that tender intimacy. This dream left me with something infinitely more valuable than just a sense of objective guidance. It touched my soul and healed me. The experience gave me both a new holistic perspective and my first glimpse of the aspect I had been overlooking. I realized that my approach to dreamwork up to that point had been like a first-grader who, in his preoccupation with sounding out words, misses the main point of the story. By focusing exclusively on decoding symbols, I had overlooked the even greater value of dreams as "feeling generators."

With this new understanding, I went back over my entries since the beginning of the experiment and found each of them to be ripe with emotional significance. One by one, I reviewed the dreams, attended to the feelings, worked with the symbols in their emotional context, and eventually came to an understanding of what each dream was generally about. Each time I discovered that the dream itself had expressed its message better than I could ever put into words. My original enthusiasm for the project returned with renewed vigor. I turned my attention to confronting the tactical problems I had been encountering and began revising my approach as needed.

The main difficulty I ran into while relying on free association was that I would often get so far off on a tangent that the original dream was all but forgotten. And because I had committed myself to working with every dream, time was also a factor. It was obvious that I would have to develop a more efficient method of approach-ing my dreams, but I was not willing to sacrifice conscientiousness for expediency. The approach I settled on would have to acknowledge feelings, content, and themes. It would need to provide guidance without becoming restrictive and be flexible enough to accommodate any dream.

I began by devising a list of questions and arranging them into a worksheet format. Most of the questions resulted from my own extensive trial and error. Gradually I began adapting suggestions from other dream explorers that I had found helpful. Even in its crude form, that first worksheet proved to be of tremendous benefit. Not only did it remind me to consider specific aspects of dreams that had resulted in valuable insights in the past, but it also provided a relatively consistent approach. With the worksheet as a guide I could continue to go off on tangents in search of a particular symbol's meaning without fear of getting lost, for I knew the point where I had departed from the path.

One of my first concerns was that a worksheet approach might dehumanize dreamwork, degrading it from an inner exploration to a mechanical process. Then I realized that because dreams are originally a spiritual experience, even encapsulating them in words results in a certain degree of distortion. Therefore the danger of dreamwork becoming mechanical is present not only with a worksheet but with *any* approach if the person involved does not closely guard against that possibility. To minimize the danger, I made innumerable revisions of the original worksheet, finally settling on the use of continuums and open-ended questions.

With the help of the revised worksheet I continued to search my dreams for meaning. From each one I learned something new that helped me to understand the dreams that followed. Many of them still appeared to be pure nonsense at first glance, of course. Many still do. But I became less inclined to regard such dreams as meaningless and more likely to conclude that I simply wasn't insightful enough to understand their meaning. Sure enough, in each case further probing would eventually bring the dream's meaning to light.

Those first hundred dreams merely whetted my appetite to learn new ways to understand their pictographic language. So I extended the research period indefinitely while continuing to revise and polish my approach. Finally, three and a half years and eight hundred dreams later, I decided that the time had come to end the experiment. I had undoubtedly done enough research to form a justifiable opinion, which had been my original intent. I was by that time convinced beyond any reasonable doubt that there is no such thing as an irrelevant or meaningless dream. Sure, I still look for that hypothetical dream without meaning and now and then I think I must have finally found it. But then someone will ask just the right question and trigger an entire chain-reaction of emotional connections that cracks the dream open and brings its meaning to light. It's like recognizing that the sun still shines even when clouds prevent me from seeing it.

There was an additional reason for ending the experiment, however. I had begun to feel as if I was "pushing the river," rather than allowing natural filtering processes to operate. While every dream may be meaningful, it does not necessarily follow that every one should be examined for meaning. Certain dreams beg to be told. Others may be more valuable when kept close to the heart. Some dreams demand that you attend to them. Still others are like weather reports that simply keep you posted on your emotional climate so you will not be surprised by a sudden storm.

Important dreams can be recognized by their intensity, mood, and recurrence. Begin by working with those. Use them like local maps on a long distance trip. Follow the one that is in your hands as far as it will take you. As you enter new territory, new maps will become available. All you need to do is be on the lookout for them.

So how often "should" you work with your dreams? That is entirely up to you. You may remember as many as several each night, but by no means would I advocate trying to work with them all. As a rule of thumb, I would not suggest trying to work with more than one or two dreams per week. That number should be more than enough to keep you well centered in the Comfort Zone. And don't worry about whether the ones you select will be meaningful; they will be. Just as they have been since that very first dream.

Chapter 4

Getting a Feel for the Dream

The Guided Interview Worksheet: Items 1-3

Have you ever noticed how some people take forever to open a birthday present? They slowly untie the ribbon, peel off the tape, carefully fold back the paper, and then ever so slowly remove and open the box while everyone in the room quivers with impatience. Then there are those who just shred the entire package in one frenzied flurry and snatch out the gift, which may or may not still be intact.

Just as there are many ways to open a present, there are also many ways of approaching a dream. The Guided Interview Worksheet evolved from a study of what dreams have in common. Its fourteen items are intended to be a framework for further exploration, not a push-button approach to dream understanding. I have tried to strike a balance between sensitivity and expediency. I don't want to splinter a dream apart with a series of emotional karate chops, but neither do I want to drag it out ad nauseam, until even the dreamer loses interest.

Despite their seemingly infinite scope of content, all dreams have recognizable common characteristics. The worksheet is a navigational chart of these reference points. Like a chart, its purpose is not to tell you where to go, but to prevent you from getting lost while exploring the deepest seas of consciousness. The worksheet can be used alone, with a partner or in a small group setting. Initially, I will be demonstrating it as it would be used by an individual. While it is often of great benefit to involve other people in the dreamwork process, there are certain precautions to consider before doing so.

These considerations will be discussed more completely in Chapter 9.

The worksheet was designed to follow dreams, not lead them. If you come to an item that does not obviously apply to your dream, feel free to skip it for the moment. If, by the end of the worksheet, you still haven't experienced the visceral sensation that says, "Oh, I get it!", go back to the items you passed by earlier and give them further consideration. As you respond to each item, ask yourself, "Does this remind me of anything that's going on in my life right now?" At any point on the worksheet, you may be struck by a particularly strong association. When that happens, by all means explore in that direction. Never feel obligated to stay with the worksheet if your dream leads you elsewhere. No matter how far you go in following a tangent, the next item will still be there on the worksheet when you get back.

Take as much time as you need when responding to any item. Remember that the object is not to get through the worksheet, but to get something out of it. At times, you may prefer to approach a dream with a single-minded focus, writing a detailed response in your journal to each item. On other occasions you might want to mull the dream over during the day like a crossword puzzle, using the worksheet as a mental bookmark.

No matter how you choose to use the Guided Interview approach, I urge you to always consider the final two items: What, if anything, would you do differently if you were to find yourself in the same dream again (item #13)? And how can you translate that solution to (or improvement upon) the dream into waking action (item #14)? Your dreams will guide you only as fast as you follow. To try to move forward without acting on previous dream understanding is like trying to climb steps of mud. Each step must be affirmed with waking action before you can make any progress.

Much of the understanding of a dream comes simply in telling it or writing it down. You may notice that I have related the examples in this book from a first-person, present-tense viewpoint. A simple exercise will help you to appreciate the benefits of doing this. First, write out a brief dream in the manner that most people tell them: as if you are recalling something that happened to you last week. Now write the same dream out again as if you are in the scene right now, voicing your thoughts and feelings about what is happening. Feel the difference?

Besides maintaining the immediacy of the dream, writing it out in the present tense also helps to fill memory gaps. Instead of trying to bring back a vague recollection of a shadowy female character, for instance, you can describe her as you see her because YOU ARE THERE. You know how you feel about her because it's all happening right in the moment. Nothing is lost. Associations will sometimes come to mind even as you tell your dream. I suggest you make note of these feelings, then set them aside. As you go through the worksheet, you may or may not find those initial impressions validated. Either way it's interesting to compare the before-and-after perspectives.

The following dream from one of my early journals illustrates how the worksheet is used. I chose this particular dream because it was recent, easily remembered, and fairly brief. When selecting a first dream of your own to work with, I suggest you use the same criteria.

> *I am standing alone at a table in a room. On it is a large, shallow pan, about the size and depth of a cookie sheet. The pan is full of rich soil, and a beautiful flower is planted in the middle. I'm trying to water the flower, but I'm having problems. No matter how carefully I try to sprinkle on the water, it washes the soil away from the roots. This happens even when I try sprinkling away from the stem at the outside edges of the pan. I realize that the soil is simply too shallow to sustain the flower. If I don't transplant it to deeper soil, the flower will have very little chance of survival.*

The first three items on the worksheet are intended to clarify the dream's content, identify the feelings generated by it and determine the urgency of the message. This section of the worksheet usually goes pretty quickly. In fact, I often use it as a shorthand method of recording middle-of-the-night dreams. In just a few minutes, I can note all of the basic information I'll need in the morning to write out a detailed version in my journal.

Item #1, which I call the SCERC outline (pronounced SKURK), appears as follows:

1) Recount the dream in the present tense, condensing the main elements into outline form:

Setting   (Describe the location, time of day, season, point in history, weather, and mood.)

Characters   (List the main characters or groups, whether they are human, animal, vegetable, or mineral.)

Event   (Essentially, what is happening in the dream?)

Response   (How do I respond to the main event? If I am not a participant in the dream, what is the response of the main character?)

Conclusion   (What is the last thing I remember happening in the dream just before awakening?)

The SCERC outline is extremely helpful in condensing long and detailed dreams into a more workable format. All of the details that are omitted during outlining are both meaningful and relevant, and will be addressed further into the worksheet. Outlining your dream, however, can enable you to recognize the larger pattern/plot which may otherwise be obscured by lesser sub-plots.

When you are listening to someone else's dream, the SCERC outline serves an additional purpose. It hones your listening skills while serving as a means of reflecting the dream back to the dreamer, thus ensuring that nothing was lost in the translation.

Begin by examining the setting of your dream. Does it take place in a familiar environment such as home, work, or school? If so, consider that the dream may be addressing concerns about that area of your life. You might want to look toward the details for further clues: If the setting is a home, is it your present one? Is it from a previous time in your life? Does it belong to a friend? Is it a home that reminds you of one you have seen in your waking life or does it exist only in your dreams?

Also note the time of day, season, and point in history when your dream takes place. Dawn has a different feeling than dusk. Spring carries connotations that winter does not. And a dream set in the fifteenth or twenty-fifth century will be significantly different from a similar dream that takes place in current times.

If the setting involves a car or other vehicle, note who is in the driver's seat, for that often reveals the person or aspect of yourself you see as currently directing your life. You also may want to note the weather in your dreamscape since weather reflects the mood of a dream. A sense of an approaching storm, for example, may be warning you to take steps to avoid upcoming difficulties. Or it could be preparing you to deal with it effectively when it arrives. If you are working with an indoor setting, try to recall whether the room felt unusually cramped or spacious and how it was lit. A very small room may be reflecting a feeling of being boxed in in some area of your life. An extremely large room, such as the interior of an airport terminal building, may be suggesting that you enjoy having room to explore without sacrificing the protection of shelter.

Sometimes, of course, an individual will report that there was no setting, or none they can remember. No problem. In that case, just try to identify the overall mood of the dream. You may also find two or more settings blending together in your dream. This is one way dreams reveal previously unrecognized similarities.

The setting in the sample dream was minimal. I initially recalled only being at a table in an otherwise empty room. But as I closed my eyes to reexperience the dream, I saw that the room in which I stood was clean, well lit, and perhaps vaguely reminiscent of some type of laboratory research area. The mood had a reflective, evaluative quality. You may note that when you are attempting to recall specific details of a dream, it is often difficult to distinguish between actual dream-memory and imagination. My advice is to be as accurate as you can, and regard any unintentional alteration of content as part of the dream. Dreams and imagination are, after all, different branches of the same tree.

Next, consider the main characters in your dream. Describe each character exactly as you experienced them in the dream such as, "loud-mouthed Mark from high school," "a wise old white-haired woman," "a ruthless mafioso dwarf named El Dido," or "my best friend, Clair." After describing them, ask yourself:

1) Do they remind me of someone in my waking life?
2) Are there times when I act like them in some way?

It is often difficult for dreamers to describe casual acquaintances or former schoolmates whom they never knew well. We're understandably reluctant to pigeon-hole someone based on so little information. But when you stop and reflect, you will find that you do have some general impression of them, even though that impression may not be entirely accurate. And they have appeared in your dream because they represent something to you.

Naturally, the characters will not always be human. You may dream of a mythical creature or a homely brown mutt. I have even worked with dreams in which the main characters were a cactus, a woodstove, and a clinging vine, respectively. In the same way that settings may blend together in a dream, the characters may be a combination of personalities or transform from one to another. Again, this is one of the ways that dreams get you to recognize common denominators.

Some dreamwork approaches list everything—and I mean EVERYTHING—as characters, and explore in detail how each represents an aspect of the dreamer. I have found such explorations to be extremely revealing on occasion and encourage you to experiment along those lines if you are so inclined. Yet they also tend to be tedious, time consuming, and generally unnecessary for my purposes. Again, the Guided Interview approach has two primary goals: 1) to elicit meaningful insights into waking situations which enable the dreamer to remain in, or return to, the Comfort Zone; and 2), to do this within a reasonable amount of time. Therefore, I generally list only the main characters.

In the sample dream, I recorded them as:

1) Myself
2) A beautiful flower (the other approach would also include the table, the dirt, the cookie sheet, et cetera as characters).

The next step is to identify the main event. Generally, when you awaken from a dream you will want to record everything you can remember about it. Yet in the very attempt to preserve it, the dream often becomes obscured in a mire of details. Although it may initially be difficult to recognize, dreams tend to have an essence: a central issue around which all sub-plots revolve. The Event in the SCERC outline should be a brief summary of this main activity. It can be likened to an overview of the forest, as opposed to an examination of individual trees.

The simplest and most effective method of identifying this central issue is to glance quickly over the dream, ignoring specifics, and ask yourself, "So basically, what's happening here?" An alternative is to try to restate the dream in the fewest possible sentences, substituting generic words such as "someone" or "something" for detailed descriptions. After boiling the dream down several times, you will eventually find a certain residue of plot remaining that can't be eliminated. This is your main event.

The Event of the sample dream could be stated as: "The survival of something beautiful is threatened by a lack of room to grow." (Again, each time you respond to a worksheet item ask yourself, "Does this remind me of anything that's currently going on in my waking life?")

After determining the dream's main event, consider your response (or the main character's response if you are only an observer) to the situation. An examination of the Response is often extremely revealing, for dream responses will candidly and accurately mirror the ways we tend to respond emotionally to waking situations.

At first glance there seemed to be no response in the sample dream. Yet, no response is still a response. By not responding to the obvious needs of the flower, I was choosing to allow the risk to escalate. Some of the most common dream responses include being paralyzed with fear or unable to make a necessary decision. I again closed my eyes to reexperience the feelings of the dream and discovered something I had not recognized earlier. While I had not actually taken action in the dream by transplanting the flower, I had resolved that I would do so. That resolution, then, could be considered the Response in Item #1.

As the final element of the SCERC outline, the Conclusion simply refers to what was happening in the dream just before you awakened. Even if the main event of the dream was not resolved, *something* was happening at that point. The conclusion of a dream generally reflects where you currently stand in terms of dealing with the issue the dream is addressing.

In the sample dream, my mere resolution to act changed nothing. The flower was still endangered when I awakened. Therefore, the Conclusion could be stated as: "Although I recognized the necessity of transplanting the flower, I have not yet taken action."

At this point, the worksheet as applied to the sample dream would appear as:

1) Setting   I'm standing at a table in a clean, well-lit, laboratory-like room.

   Characters   Myself and the flower.

   Event   The survival of something beautiful is threatened by a lack of room to grow.

   Response   I resolve to transplant the flower.

   Conclusion   Though I recognize the necessity of transplanting the flower, I have not yet taken action.

When I'm teaching a dream class, much of the first evening is spent in discussing recall strategies. By the second or third meeting, however, I'm more likely to be bombarded by students waving dreams that are several pages long and complaining they don't know what to do with it all. This is where the SCERC outline becomes valuable. It reduces the dream to its essence and makes it less intimidating to work with.

The SCERC outline, ending with the conclusion of the dream, leads directly into the second item on the worksheet:

2) **At the conclusion of the dream, I experienced feelings that I would plot on an emotional spectrum as:**

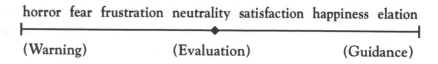

Although many feelings may be experienced during the course of a single dream, the worksheet specifically focuses on the feelings that immediately precede awakening. It's like riding a city bus; though you'll undoubtedly make several stops along the way, the one that matters most is the stop where you get off. In the same way, because the feelings at the conclusion are the ones you were left with, they are the most useful in understanding the purpose of the dream. If you have trouble in recalling these feelings, a quick trip back into the dream will usually bring them forth quite easily. Close your eyes if you find it helps you to concentrate. After you have reexperienced your emotional state at the conclusion of the dream, plot a point on the worksheet that most closely represents the main feeling.

Just below the spectrum line you will find three words: "Warning, Evaluation, and Guidance." These categories represent three general types of dreams. By looking beneath the point that was plotted, you can determine the category into which your dream primarily falls. For instance, at the conclusion of the sample dream I was feeling frustrated in my unsuccessful attempts to water the flower and concerned for its survival. These feelings of frustration and concern would be plotted somewhere just to the left of center on the emotional spectrum. This suggests to me that the dream is essentially an evaluation, but also contains a certain degree of warning. So who cares? What possible good does it do to categorize a dream?

The first step in getting out of prison is to realize that you are, in fact, imprisoned. And you are unlikely to recover a buried treasure if you are not first aware that such a treasure exists. In the same way, I'm better able to act wisely upon a dream when I understand what type of dream it is and whether I'm looking for a warning or a suggestion.

It's helpful to recognize Warning Dreams when they first appear. At that point, they are still in the subtle stage, leaving you with only a vague feeling of frustration or disappointment. This is by far the easiest time to face them and discover what it is they are warning you about. If you do not heed these early warnings, they are likely to escalate in intensity to get your attention, sometimes even catapulting you awake with the original primal scream. Although these nightmarish dreams are generally more difficult to acknowledge, they can be some of the most helpful you will ever have. In the first place, their symbolism is bold and distinct, as opposed to the subtle, enigmatic images of milder dreams. These easily identifiable feelings generally make the dreams simpler to unravel. Secondly, these dreams provide clear cut advance warnings that, if heeded, can prevent you from making serious mistakes. *Bear in mind that disturbing dreams do not cause problems. They merely alert you to existing problems.* Once you realize this, acknowledge the dreams—however painful—and take steps to alter your present course, these dreams can be extremely beneficial.

Ironically, many people try to shut out Warning Dreams for fear that to acknowledge them would open a Pandora's Box of recurrent terrors. In truth, these dreams are like red traffic signals: only dangerous when ignored. Unfortunately, many of us have a remarkable ability to ignore our own discomfort. Sure, we complain, but our complaints are often just a way of adapting to what we consider an "acceptable" level of misery in our lives. At the same time, we often overestimate the sacrifice involved in initiating the necessary changes. One function of a Warning Dream, then, might be to motivate you into action by making you more afraid of where you are than of where you need to go. As you begin to make progress, your dreams will naturally become less disturbing.

In comparison to those in the warning category, Evaluation Dreams are tame. In fact, they are characterized by their very lack of strong feelings. In many of these, the dreamer is an observer rather than a participant, and may have the detached feeling of viewing the situation from an objective viewpoint. Evaluation Dreams essentially provide an overview of the dreamer's current life in much the same way that a traffic helicopter can guide you to the clearest route home during rush hour. What you are looking for in these dreams, then, is an indication of what that clearest route might be.

The dreams that fall into the third category, Guidance, tend to be everyone's favorites. These are the ones you wish would last forever. They allow you to touch the sublime and see first hand that there is, indeed, a treasure worth digging for. It's easy to recognize the feeling of a Guidance Dream, although they too, vary in intensity. Some are like a warm bath on a winter morning that leaves you feeling wonderfully relaxed and at peace. In others, a sense of ecstasy may lift you into a transcendent state of mind where you realize that existence simply cannot get any better. Guidance Dreams are a good indication that there are opportunities currently available in your waking life. When working with these dreams, be on special lookout for clues that might help identify waking opportunities from which you could benefit.

The next item on the worksheet involves the vividness or intensity of the dream. Item #3 appears on the worksheet as follows:

3) On a scale of 1-10, I would rate the vividness/intensity of this dream as:

```
    0    1    2    3    4    5    6    7    8    9    10
    ├─────────────────────────◆─────────────────────────┤
  (green)                 (ripening)              (ripe)
```

Dreams that leave the dreamer with a powerful impression are generally described as either "vivid" or "intense," depending upon whether the experience was pleasant or disturbing. The scale in item #3 on the worksheet uses the terms synonymously to depict the extent to which the dreamer was affected by the dream. I sometimes call this the "Ripeness Scale," since a dream that powerfully affects the dreamer suggests there are ripe issues in his or her waking life that require immediate attention. A dream of lesser intensity reflects that the issue being addressed is "greener," or not as fully developed.

You might want to respond to a mild Warning Dream, for example, by taking corrective measures before the lightweight difficulty escalates into a heavyweight problem. Similarly, a mild Guidance

Dream might serve as an inspiration to take some sort of affirmative waking action that will help bring your heart's desire a step closer to physical manifestation. As dreams ripen, or the level of vividness/intensity increases, the need to take either corrective or affirmative action becomes proportionately more important.

In the sample dream, I was deeply concerned about the possible loss of something very precious to me. I rated the vividness/intensity of this dream at somewhere around seven on the ripeness scale. This indicated to me that the dream was addressing a fairly urgent issue. That realization inspired me to find out what the dream was about so I could make necessary corrections before the issue evolved any further.

If dreams are the compass that leads you back to the Comfort Zone, then the Guided Interview Worksheet is the navigational chart. Used together, they offer invaluable guidance no matter what your objective may be. If you want to run quickly through the feeling of your dream just to see what the emotional weather is like, you can do that. If you prefer to pull out the chart and explore each area in depth, that too, is your prerogative.

As you become familiar with the worksheet, your responses will rarely take very long. It is like recording your initial impressions of a stranger. First you note the general appearance of your dream, then you get a feeling about its basic personality. Finally you determine whether it is more of a casual encounter or likely to develop into a deeper involvement.

Chapter 5

Locating the Heart of the Dream

The Guided Interview Worksheet: Items 4-6

Just as initial impressions are only the first step in getting to know someone, acquiring a feel for a dream is only the beginning of understanding it. The next section of the worksheet probes further in hopes of refining the main event of the dream into a recognizable issue. The best way to begin is to give the dream a short title. A good title can crystallize an entire dream into just a few words. Titling appears on the worksheet as item #4:

4) In about 5 words, write a title that reflects the essence of your dream (refer to the Event in the SCERC outline).

Title: _____

There are several excellent reasons for titling your dreams. One is that titling helps to more easily identify and locate recurrent themes. Say, for instance, you are writing down a dream in which several of your teeth fell out. Suddenly, you remember having a nearly identical dream just last month. Or was it last summer? As your dream collection grows, you will discover that it is much easier to glance through a list of titles than to reread an entire stack of journals—especially if you have put enough thought into the titles to have them reflect the essence of your dreams. A less utilitarian motive for titling your dreams is to show that you value them. After all, we rarely name things unless we care about them. And caring about your dreams will lead you to a deeper understanding of their wisdom.

There are usually several good title possibilities for a dream. Try to pick one that best expresses its essence or irony. For the sample dream, a good title might be "Flower In A Shallow Pan." It's short, it captures the irony of the image, and even hidden among a long list of titles, would easily remind me of this particular dream. With the title helping me to maintain a clear image of the dream in my mind, I'm ready to move on to the next item.

Many dreams present situations the dreamer would prefer to avoid. It may be as passive as averting a look from a haggard or disfigured character or as active as an escape from an angry mob. Either way, the very fact that it is being avoided suggests a significance worthy of closer inspection. Item #5 examines the matter of avoidance.

5) Was there anything in the dream I was avoiding? If so, what was it and why was it important that I avoid it?

Anything you refuse to face in waking life will follow you across the bridge into sleep. There you can continue to try to avoid it, but avoidance in the dream state is both more difficult and more obvious. Dreams intentionally bring such issues to your awareness. As with any uncomfortable situation, it is much easier to acknowledge the issue in its early stages than wait for it to escalate. A dream depicting casual avoidance serves as a gentle reproach that you have been neglecting something that needs attention. At this stage, I would recommend that you study the dream to discover the significance of the character or situation you are avoiding. Once recognized, you can then take waking actions to correct your oversight. There is also the possibility, of course, that you may act upon the dream without even realizing you have done so. In either case, the issue would be resolved and your dreams would turn their attention to other matters.

There are times, however, when a dream presents a scenario that the dreamer steadfastly refuses to acknowledge. This refusal to face difficult or frightening situations sets the stage for "Chase Dreams." In these dreams, something is pursuing you. You flee because you are convinced it would be harmful, even suicidal, to do otherwise. You may successfully escape only to discover later that your freedom was no more than a temporary reprieve, for unconfronted Chase Dreams almost always lead to more of the same. As the theme recurs, you will be forced to either repeat your escape against increasingly difficult odds, or finally to turn and face your aggressor. Since the dreams have a purpose, they will not go away until you either consciously acknowledge and act upon the dream, or are gradually influenced by the dreams to make necessary changes in your waking life. Unattended, these dreams can recur over periods of years. An alternative is to intentionally confront the dreams and reduce the process to a fraction of that time. You may even end a series of Chase Dreams on the spot. Again, your choices make all the difference.

While it does seem to be a fact that the only way to end a Chase Dream permanently is to brave the danger, confrontation does not mean choosing between death and surrender. Dream confrontations can take many forms. Violent confrontations are generally more satisfying to the dreamer than continued avoidance. But in dreams, as in waking life, violence begets violence. As a result, pursuit and violent confrontation themes may persist for quite some time before the situation improves. Another option is nonviolent confrontation. In these dreams, understanding overcomes opposition; integration replaces aggression. You may simply stand your ground, refusing to either run from or bow to the aggressor. You might ask the aggressor what it wants, or why it is chasing you. Although logic dictates that to choose this option would mean certain death, that logic does not take into consideration the fact that dreams have a purpose. They are trying to get you to face an issue. Once you confront the issue portrayed by the dream aggressor, the dream's purpose is served. At that point, the dream aggressor is generally transformed into a more amiable character. My experience has overwhelmingly convinced me that nonviolent confrontations are by far the most effective way to end Chase Dreams.

I realize that I am discussing confrontations as if it were possible to initiate them intentionally within the dream state. In fact, it is. Although it may come as a bit of a surprise, it is nevertheless quite possible to make conscious choices within your dreams. This you will undoubtedly discover for yourself during your own dream explorations. The vast implications and exciting possibilities of intentional dreaming will be discussed at length in chapter ten, including specific methods and techniques. Of course, aggressors are not always faced within the dream state. But you can still confront them with equal effectiveness through waking dreamwork. This approach will be detailed in the next two chapters.

If there is something being avoided in a dream, you generally won't have to look very hard to find it. If you do detect evasion at any point in a dream, be sure to draw it out and look at it more closely. It is very likely to be the key to understanding your dream. In "Flower In A Shallow Pan," however, avoidance was apparently not a significant issue.

The next item probably requires more contemplation than anything else on the worksheet, but it is well worth the effort for it will lead you directly to the heart of the dream. Just as every child is born of the union of two complementary aspects, so is every dream. If you want to understand the essence of a child, look to that child's parents. And when you are searching for the essence of a dream, look for the "polarities" of that dream. The polarities of a dream often appear, either explicitly or implicitly, as a choice. That choice is considered in item #6, which appears as follows on the worksheet:

6) **In this dream, the choice is:**
    Conformity vs. Individuality   **Decisiveness vs. Acquiescence**
    Abundance vs. Need   **Honesty vs. Deception**
    Freedom vs. Restriction   **Desires vs. Loyalties**
    Separation vs. Reunion   **Power vs. Impotence**
    Privacy vs. Exposure   **Death vs. Rebirth**
    Vulnerability vs. Toughness   **Confrontation vs. Avoidance**
    Imbalance vs. Equilibrium   **Commitment vs. Desertion**
    Or: _____vs. _____

The polarities listed in item #6 cover most of the common choices encountered in dreams. The list is by no means absolute, and you may word your choices quite differently. Still, it is often helpful to use the list as a starting point. You may discover that one pair of polarities basically fits your dream, but the wording is not quite right. In that case, reword the choice until it mirrors your dream as closely as possible. Although some dreams seem to contain more than one pair of polarities, there is usually one that resonates more strongly than the others. That's the one to look at.

To recognize a dream's polarities, or its choice, is to come as close as possible to touching the true spirit of the dream. This is especially helpful when examining a series of dreams that occur on a single night. Same-night series often address a single issue from a variety of perspectives. Although the dreams may seem to have little or nothing in common in terms of characters, images or events, they often share the same basic choice. That is the clue that reveals their common parentage.

In trying to determine the basic choice being presented in "Flower In A Shallow Pan," I first glanced over the list of polarities. The dream contained an element of "Freedom vs. Restriction" in that the full potential of the flower was being restricted by an inadequate environment. "Commitment vs. Desertion" also seemed to apply to a certain extent, for I was faced with either caring for the flower or just walking away. After careful consideration, I decided the most fundamental choice was between giving the flower a new birth by transplanting it, or allowing it to die. Of the polarities listed, "Death vs. Rebirth" seemed to come closest to reflecting the primary choice of the dream. Still, I wasn't quite satisfied with the wording. I finally settled on "Relocation vs. Slow Death" as my response to the sixth item.

Items 4 through 6 on the worksheet go beyond the surface details of the dream and touch its very heart. Titling the dream crystallizes its essence, making it easier to keep in mind and recognize at a later date. Acknowledging avoidance in a dream makes the dreamer aware of waking issues he or she may have been overlooking. And by looking deeply into the dream for the polarities from which it was born, the heart of the dream begins to come into focus.

This is how the second portion of the Guided Interview Worksheet would appear as applied to "Flower In A Shallow Pan":

4) Title: *Flower In A Shallow Pan*
5) (Avoidance does not appear to be a significant issue.)
6) In this dream, the choice is between: *Relocation vs. Slow Death*

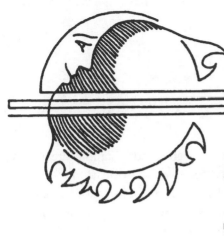

Chapter 6

Looking from the Inside Out

The Guided Interview Worksheet: Items 7-10

Throughout the first half of the worksheet, the sample dream was essentially captured and tagged for easy identification. Now it's time to release it back into the wild where we can follow it and see where it leads us. The trail begins with an overview of outstanding images and a closer look at the characters who populate our dreams. Then we'll be projecting into the dream and exploring the feelings from an insider's perspective.

There is a great deal to be learned from the symbolic images of dreams. It has been my experience that every dream image is meaningful. Nothing is coincidental or included at random. Often, the large number of images or symbols appearing in a dream make it virtually impossible to work with each one. For that reason, I generally select only the most outstanding ones, as they tend to be the most revealing. These key images, addressed in item #7, will be your guides along the next leg of the journey.

7) **List the most outstanding images that appeared in the dream, along with a brief statement defining and describing each.**

There are several good techniques that can help you to understand the significance of a specific dream image. But before discussing them, I feel a responsibility to caution against over reliance upon symbols alone. In the first place, as I discovered in my own initial attempts at understanding dreams, a dream is more than the sum of its parts. Interpretation based solely upon the translation of symbols is dry, lifeless, and often misleading. The other problem overlooked by the many "dream dictionaries" on the market is that there simply are no truly universal symbols.

As human beings and planetary shipmates, we all share certain common elemental things that may be reflected in our dreams. Citizens of individual countries might have somewhat more in common by sharing a national heritage and geography. The smaller the group, be it cultural, religious, or family, the more they will have in common. As a result, there may be many shared dream symbols. But even same sex identical twins raised in a common household will each have their own independent life experiences, resulting in unique symbolic associations. One may be fascinated by honeybees, for instance, while the other may have a strong fear of them. The point is that dream images must be explored in relation to the dreamer's own individual background. Personal associations always take precedence over cultural connotations.

All effective techniques for unveiling dream symbolism share one basic goal: to enable the dreamer to describe an image from their subjective point of view rather than from conditioned preconceptions or popularly accepted meanings. Many cultures, for example, commonly regard dogs as "man's best friend." A dreamer who has been attacked by a dog, however, or an Asian dreamer who considers dogs a part of the cuisine are likely to have very different associations. The part of you that creates your dreams specifically chooses images that are meaningful to you in order to send an intimately personal message. One way to understand that message, then, is to get back in touch with your personal feelings about the images.

There are several methods of doing this. Some dreamers find it helpful to describe the image as if they were introducing it to a visitor from another planet who is entirely unfamiliar with Earth culture. Another approach uses role playing. In this instance, the dreamer assumes the viewpoint of the enigmatic image (this can be done even if the dream image is an inanimate object) and allows the image to describe itself from a first-person perspective. If you are fortunate enough to have friends who share your interest in dreamwork, you may want to try yet another technique.

After sharing your dream aloud, have your friends take turns adopting the dream as their own. As they describe their associations with what they consider to be the most outstanding images, you sit quietly with paper and pen. Make note of any of your friends' associations that resonate within you and disregard any that do not. This approach can be helpful in priming the pump if you are unable to spontaneously come up with any meaning on your own. Of course, some dreams are so intimate and personal that you may not want to invite other people to tromp around in them. This, along with the other pros and cons of group dreamwork, will be addressed more fully in chapter nine.

Another critical factor in understanding dream images is the context within which they appear. When viewed outside that framework, the images may have little or no relevance. One association with the image of a kiss, for instance, might be: "tenderness, a special intimate connection, an expression of love." Yet the kiss of a lover has very little, if anything, in common with kissing the Pope's ring, or a mobster's "Kiss of Death." The symbolism of an image must always be considered within the context of the dream.

Take any path you choose to arrive at a subjectively accurate description of your outstanding images. Pay special attention to details that make the images unique. If you dream of French raisin bread, note how it differs from other varieties of bread. Since associations with dream images can easily become lengthy, try to condense your descriptions down to a few key words or phrases before listing them on the worksheet. And remember, after describing any image, ask yourself that vital question, "Does this remind me of anything in my current life?" Make note of any mental connections and follow them up before proceeding with the worksheet.

Compared to many dreams, "Flower In A Shallow Pan" had a very stark dreamscape. Even so, there were at least four key images with which to work:

Laboratory-like room = A place where experiments are carried out for educational and practical purposes.

Large, shallow pan = Appears spacious at first glance but has little depth.

(This association resulted in a strong emotional connection to my work situation at the time of the dream. Although my duties were varied and interesting, I never felt deeply involved in the work.)

Rich soil = Although the quality of the soil is good, it doesn't go deep enough to sustain the flower. Rich soil or not, the flower is dying.

(Here again, I was reminded of my work situation. Despite a comfortable salary, my needs for personal/spiritual growth were not being satisfied. This new understanding made the remaining dream image easy to recognize.)

The flower = Something of rare beauty, alive and growing, very special and important to me.

(At this point, I had no doubt that the flower represented my personal/spiritual growth.)

The link between a dream and waking reality rarely is revealed merely by defining or describing the dream images. It is instead the emotional connections that occur while arriving at those descriptions that make the link obvious. That does not mean you will always have strong feelings about every image you describe. In the sample dream, for instance, I initially felt no connection with the "laboratory-like room." Later, though, I was sharing insights I had gotten from the dream with my wife. As we discussed my work situation, I happened to comment that I had originally taken the job, "...as a sort of experiment." Suddenly the last piece of the puzzle fell into place and I realized that the setting of the dream had been perfectly appropriate.

The feelings that surfaced as I described the key images brought powerful new meaning to the choice presented in the dream between "Relocation & Slow Death." Something within me strongly resonated to the idea that my work situation was providing insufficient nourishment for my soul. The emotional connections, along with the insights uncovered earlier in the worksheet, gradually developed into a clear picture of the waking situation that was being reflected in the dream. These clues spurred me on to discover more details, get more closely in touch with my feelings on the matter, and decide upon an appropriate course of action.

In the next item, dream characters are given an opportunity to express their perspectives and motivations in their own manner. Observed on their home turf, dream characters reveal the countless mixed feelings that continually struggle for recognition within us all. Only by viewing the dreamscape through the various characters' own eyes can we begin to appreciate the validity of the factors that have shaped their unique perspectives.

Even the attempt to give fair consideration to these diverse viewpoints is a valuable first step in resolving long standing inner conflicts. An effective way to do this is briefly to assume the role of each main character and allow them to make a statement, as shown in item #8 below.

8) **First, list the parties or groups involved in the main event. Next, write a short "motto" for each that represents the basic viewpoint of that character or group.**

	Participants		Mottos
a)	_____	=	_____
b)	_____	=	_____
c)	_____	=	_____

Examples of mottos are the Boy Scout adage, "Be Prepared," or Pollyanna's "Always look for something good in everything that happens." When establishing a motto for the participants in your dream, it is essential that you do so from each character's own viewpoint. Since every participant or group is unique, no two mottos should be alike. Ideally, a motto will answer the question, "Where is this character coming from?" It will allow you to discover how the character sees himself and why he acts the way he does. By allowing the character to speak for himself, you avoid the common mistake of making a judgmental statement and assuming it represents the character's own point of view. A good way to test the validity of a motto is to ask, "Would this character agree with the motto I have given him? Is it something he would express himself?" A positive reply to these questions will ensure that you have captured the essence of the character.

Occasionally, as with the flower in the sample dream, something can be regarded as both a key image and a main character. That presents no problem. Just view the image from both perspectives. Also, the participants may be groups rather than individuals. In that case, you would strive to create a motto that reflects the guiding principles or basic beliefs of each group. It is often helpful to focus on leader or representative of the group and then let that representative establish a motto for the group.

Although giving voice to dream characters is a bit like the phenomenon called "channeling," it draws more on the child within you than the psychic. Have fun with it. Don't think about it too much. Just pretend you are the character and say whatever it is you want to say to the world. Like a child at play, learn to become a bad guy one minute and a good guy the next. This is the kind of flexibility needed, for dreamwork requires you to see through the eyes of heroes and villains alike. Sometimes you may even find that one character wants to respond to the motto of another. Let it happen. Impromptu "dialogues" between dream characters often lead to enlightening realizations.

The sample dream contains two main participants: myself and the flower. I want my motto to express my strongest feelings and motivations in this specific dream, rather than one that attempts to encompass my entire life philosophy. Again, I closed my eyes to return to the dream and searched for the best possible way to express my feelings accurately and concisely. My response on the worksheet read:

"I am the flower's caretaker. I genuinely want it to flourish and would feel terrible if it died."

That one simple statement resulted in an abrupt shift of perception. Whereas I had initially observed the flower with detachment and objectivity, my feelings suddenly became profoundly personal. I realized with some surprise that I cared very deeply about what happened to the flower.

But what about the other side of the story? How did the flower feel about its predicament? In order to experience the flower's point of view, I needed to temporarily become that flower. I first envisioned the flower, then imagined myself experiencing reality through its senses. As a flower, I felt my needs and desires welling up as a desperate plea from within and wrote:

"PLEASE move me to where my roots can spread out! I want to become everything I can be."

A good motto will not just stick in your mind, it will resonate in your gut. The resonance of the flower's motto let me know I had touched something real.

Sometimes while voicing a character's motto you will recognize a familiar figure of speech often used by someone well known to you in waking life. Even certain tones of voice may open a door that leads you further toward an understanding of your dream. Say, for instance, you recognize your Aunt Dottie's favorite expression in the motto of one of your characters. Consider not only what Aunt Dottie might have to do with your current situation, but also how you might be acting like Aunt Dottie in it.

Item #9 focuses in on the most potent moment of your dream and freezes it in time. This grants you the time and space to safely examine this emotional turning point more closely. It is expressed on the worksheet as follows:

9) **Draw a simple sketch, or describe a "mental snapshot" of the most emotionally highly-charged scene in the dream.**

Please note that the wording is "simple sketch," not "timeless masterpiece." Naturally, I wouldn't want to discourage you from creating a work of art based upon your dream. But if your artistic talent is limited to mapping things out with stick figures, I don't want that to discourage you either. Since most dreams are primarily visual, drawing them out even roughly will often bring you closer to the original experience. Some dreamers enjoy making collages from magazine photos and clippings. If you are short of time or materials are not available, just recreate the scene as vividly as possible in your mind. Describe it as if it were one frozen frame of a motion picture. Don't intellectualize it. Just project yourself into that one scene and relate what you see firsthand.

In the most highly-charged scene from "Flower In A Shallow Pan," I was leaning over the table, gently sprinkling water on the base of the flower. Despite my care, the soil kept washing away and exposing the roots. I decided to sketch it.

Watering The Flower

While responding to item #10, continue to imagine yourself in the scene just drawn or visualized in the previous item. Complete the following statement from your perspective within that reconstructed scene:

10) **Mentally project yourself into the scene you just drew. After the words, "I feel...," write at least three words that describe your state of emotion.**

   "I feel...":

Make certain you respond to the statement with *feelings* rather than thoughts. "I'm excited about..." is a feeling. "I'm wondering if..." is a thought. Learn to recognize the difference. You may venture off onto some interesting tangents by intellectualizing, but it is your feelings that are most likely to lead to an understanding of your dream.

In "Flower In A Shallow Pan," I responded to item #10 as follows:

"I feel...": *concerned, anxious, and frustrated that I can't properly nourish the flower to its fullest potential.*

Throughout this section of the worksheet, the dream is given free rein. You will generally reap the most benefit by approaching these items playfully, with an attitude of lighthearted reverence. By literally "getting into" the characters and images, you can experience the dream from a variety of perspectives. This is crucial if you want to understand the motivations of characters to whom you have initial difficulty in relating. Only by giving your dream characters an opportunity to express themselves without restraint can you recognize the validity of their viewpoint. This willingness to consider new outlooks will result not only in the discovery of profound truths from the most unlikely sources, but will also immeasurably broaden your overall perspective.

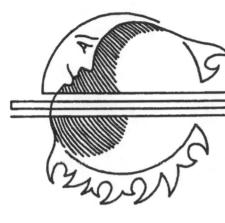

Chapter 7

The Link between Realities

The Guided Interview Worksheet: Items 11-14

Dreams do not exist in a vacuum. Neither does your physical life. Both continually interrelate and play upon each other in countless ways. The aim of the final section of the worksheet is to reveal the sinuous connections between these various levels of consciousness. It is designed to help you understand better the hidden reasons behind your waking experience. These last four items will help you to decide exactly where you would like to go with your life and what actions can be taken to get you there. This is the practical phase of dreamwork. It's not enough merely to recognize the waking situation your dream is reflecting and leave it at that. Your dreams occur with the purpose of influencing your waking actions in ways that will benefit your life.

The eleventh item reexamines the feelings you listed as your response to the statement in item #10 ("I feel..."). It appears on the worksheet in the following form:

11) In what kinds of WAKING situations have I had feelings similar to those just described in item #10?

When responding to this item, keep in mind that you are looking for a similarity of *feelings*, not events. When I considered this item in regard to "Flower In A Shallow Pan," for instance, I was not interested in the last time I planted a flower or was alone in a laboratory-like room. Instead I asked, "When in my waking life have I felt concerned, anxious, and frustrated?" Phrased in this way, the question evoked an immediate visceral reaction. Those words precisely described how I had been feeling about my employment situation. Although this was not entirely new material, it reaffirmed intuitions that had come to me in earlier stages of the dreamwork.

Occasionally, instead of flashing on one specific situation in response to this item, you may think of several circumstances in which the feelings apply. This is particularly common when working with a recurring dream. In cases like these, look for a common denominator in all the situations that come to mind. A pattern will usually appear.

While working with a dream of his own, a student named George described his feelings in response to item #10 as: anger, fear, and resentment. His initial reply to item #11 was, "There are a lot of times when I feel that way—like when my boss moved a deadline up on me, or when my sister and her family came to visit and expected me to entertain them all week, or even when panhandlers ask me for money." Later, while searching for a common denominator in all those situations, George noticed that in each one he felt obligated to do something he did not want to do, yet acquiesced in spite of his feelings. That realization proved to be the turning point in his understanding of the dream.

When attempting to understand a dream it is essential to consider when, where, and under what circumstances the dream took place. This waking life context is the focus of item #12, as shown below:

12) **What was most strongly on my mind before going to sleep? Or, what is the primary concern in my life at this time and what specific obstacles are in my path?**

If you made a predream entry, this is a good time to review it. If you did not make a predream entry and find it difficult to view your current situation objectively, try relating it in the third person as if you were a reporter writing an article about your circumstances. Mention your age, sex, marital and occupational status, and a brief description of recent waking events.

Dreams can always be depended upon to filter through the barrage of issues in your life and focus upon those that are currently top priority items. When your dream depicts past situations it is because the issues that were going on then are somehow emotionally linked to your present circumstances. The same is true when you dream of characters or events from a television program you watched just before bedtime. Your dreams are non-partisan. They will borrow emotionally potent materials from any source and weave them into a unique dream that fits your personal needs. What this all means is that by becoming more aware of emotionally charged issues in your daily life, you are more likely to understand your dreams. It is even possible to refine a particularly pressing concern into a "request" and intentionally dream about that chosen subject. Requests will be addressed along with intentional dreaming in chapter ten.

At the time I dreamed "Flower In A Shallow Pan," I was living in Miami, Florida. My wife and I had moved there from a small town in Colorado a little more than two years earlier to participate in a project we felt had great social value. At first, my involvement gave me a strong sense of purpose. After the completion of the project's main goal, however, that sense of purpose began to wane. What I had originally done out of strong commitment I found myself doing just because it was a steady job. I considered leaving, but lacked the strong motivation that had originally fueled our cross-country move.

As frequently happens, these predream concerns clearly mirrored my response to item #11 (linking waking situations to feelings experienced in the dream). A similarity between these two items is always a strong verification that you are on the right track in the pursuit of your dream's meaning. If, on the other hand, your predream entry bears little or no resemblance to the results of item #11, it does not necessarily mean you are on the wrong track. You may recognize the issue being presented in the dream as one that has been in the back of your mind but had not been addressed consciously until the dream brought it to your attention. As you exercise your intuitive muscles through the practice of dreamwork, you probably will begin to notice your predream entries becoming increasingly perceptive and therefore more closely aligned with your responses to item #11.

In the next item, we will be taking liberties with the dream content through what I call "redreaming" and "paradreaming." Dreams, after all, are not chiseled in stone but are instead mental patterns that can yet be altered. This is NOT the same as pretending that a disturbing dream never happened. Nor is it intended to be a way to avoid experiencing the trauma, pain, and sorrow that dreams can sometimes bring to light. Only after you have fully acknowledged the original feelings of the dream should you consider redreaming or paradreaming. At that point, however, these mental exercises can be invaluable in helping to consciously create and reinforce new thought patterns. Item #13 appears on the worksheet as follows:

13) If I were to have this same dream again tonight, what (if anything) would I do differently to create a more satisfying outcome?

   a) ("Redreaming") Alter the sketch you made in response to item #9, incorporating any change you would like to make.

   b) ("Paradreaming") If the conclusion of your dream was completely satisfying, consider what you would have liked to have happen next, had you not awakened when you did.

There is a great deal to be discovered by comparing what actually happened in a dream to what you would have liked to have happen. The former reveals where things currently stand in your waking life and the latter gives a clue as to where you would like to go from here. This is your opportunity to be wildly creative. If you had a disturbing dream, list every imaginable alternative, even those that seem absurd or impossible. Do NOT think interpretively at this point. Just have fun with it. Your imagination and ingenuity are the most valuable tools you possess. Perhaps instead of being swallowed by that dream alligator, you could have used one of your shoelaces to tie its mouth shut. Never mind that it wouldn't work in the Everglades—anything is possible in your dreams!

Don't assume you need to come up with a perfect solution to every dilemma. Maybe some dilemmas don't have perfect solutions. In that case, just try for an improvement. Consider every angle as you list possible alternatives to the original dream content: Where are you right now in the dream? Where do you want to be? Whom do you want to be with? What obstacles are in the way? What can you do to overcome those obstacles? Once you have listed several possible changes, select a few of your favorites. Play each out to its ultimate conclusion in your mind. You may come up with some surprising realizations.

I once worked with a dream told to me by a young woman named Nicki. She related how it had begun in her home and, through a series of misadventures, developed into a frightening Chase Dream. When I later asked her what she would do differently if she were to have the dream again, she half-jokingly replied, "I would have never left my house!" I encouraged her to play out that option in her mind and see how it felt. After briefly contemplating it, she laughed and said, "It feels boring. I think I'd rather be chased than to just sit around the house all the time!" This recognition of her need for excitement deepened her understanding of the original dream and opened up new avenues in her thinking. By exploring them, Nicki was able to come up with several alternative ways of bringing excitement into her life that would have more enjoyable consequences.

Contrary to what many people believe, not all dreams are unpleasant. If your original dream was delightful and there is nothing you would have done differently to alter the outcome, imagine it continuing past the point at which you awakened. This is what I call paradreaming. It is a method of helping you to discover the necessary next steps in bringing your favorite dreams to life.

While redreaming or paradreaming, always keep in mind that this is your fantasy and you can lead it in any direction you choose. If you are worried that fantasy has nothing to do with your day-to-day existence, don't be. In the final item on the worksheet you will be delineating specific steps that can be taken to make your heart's wishes a reality.

As I redreamed "Flower In A Shallow Pan," it was immediately apparent that if I did nothing the flower would surely die. I initially envisioned transplanting it into a large flowerpot and keeping it indoors as a houseplant. That still felt too restrictive. Finally, the perfect spot came to mind; a sheltered area in a large yard, surrounded by lush vegetation. I visualized planting the flower in rich, loamy soil where all its needs would be met naturally and it would have unlimited room to grow.

An invaluable step in physically manifesting any new idea is putting it on paper. This is true whether you are building a house, designing a machine, or even cultivating a new habit. In item #9 you have already created the scene as it actually existed in the dream. Now recreate it as you would like it to be. Using your favorite medium, reproduce the scene you selected for item #13 ("If I were to have this same dream again tonight..."). It makes little difference if you paint it, make a magazine collage, build it out of construction paper and cardboard, or just vividly imagine it. Spontaneity and emotional appeal are more important than aesthetics. Persevere until it is emotionally satisfying. Later, when you lie down to go to sleep, envision the revised scene in as much detail as possible for about five minutes. Then let it go. It usually will not be long before you begin to see elements of the new pattern appearing in your dreams.

Below is the revised sketch I drew for "Flower In A Shallow Pan."

Transplanting The Flower

I hope you will by now have at least a general impression of the waking life issue being addressed by your dream. If not, just keep it in the back of your mind for a day or two. Given a little time and space, associations may begin to surface. Naturally, you won't always "get" every dream that comes to you. Don't let that bother you. The theme will recur until it has nudged you back toward the Comfort Zone. And even when you are unable to recognize the connections between your dreaming and waking realities, you are still exercising your problem-solving skills through the practice of dreamwork.

This brings us to the final item on the worksheet, #14, which involves finding ways to translate these changes into physical terms. It appears as follows:

14) How can I translate these dream improvements into waking terms I can act upon TODAY to similarly improve my physical situation?

During the preceding exercise you visualized, and perhaps put on paper, changes or additions to your original dream. This in itself is often tremendously satisfying. But an even greater sense of fulfillment comes as you translate your new understanding into action. No dreamwork is complete until some form of physical action is taken, based upon a combination of dream guidance and practical waking considerations. As a rule, it is better to consistently take small, conservative dream-based actions than to change your entire life impulsively on the basis of a single dream. Yet some people are reluctant to take any action at all, for fear they have not "correctly" interpreted their dream.

This is an understandable concern. Verification of dream insights is purely subjective and can only be resolved by the dreamer. Listed below are three questions that can help you determine the validity of your interpretation.

1) Do I feel a physical, gut-level affirmation of the dreamwork?

How do you know when you are excited? Or afraid? Or angry? You feel it in your body. That is also the best way to determine the accuracy of your dreamwork. You might sense an inner "click" or "Aha!" that lets you know you have touched something real. You may even experience goosebumps rising on your arms or a shiver up your spine. Associations that intellectually make sense to you but lack this type of physiological resonance are not likely to be of much value.

2) Does the dreamwork reveal something new?

Never settle for a mere rehash of previously known information. Dreams come to enlighten. If a dream seems to be presenting you with situations already familiar to you, look deeper. There is something you have missed.

3) Do subsequent dreams reflect increased harmony and equilibrium?

This question ultimately tests not only your understanding of a dream, but also your incorporation of that understanding. Say, for instance, you have come up with what appear to be valid insights into a Chase Dream. But then the following night your dreams contain chase elements of even greater intensity. That would be a pretty clear indication that you either misunderstood the original dream or failed to incorporate the understanding into your daily life. This is one of the many wonderful traits of dreams: they are self-correcting. If you have misunderstood the basic message, your dreams themselves will dependably point out the error. An accurate interpretation, on the other hand, will guide you back toward the sanctuary of the Comfort Zone. This, too, will become apparent in subsequent dreams.

Before dreaming "Flower In A Shallow Pan," I had already been aware of a growing dissatisfaction with my work situation. Yet I had only considered the practical and economic aspects. From that viewpoint alone, it did not seem advisable to abandon a stable situation. Yet the dream brought to my attention that a failure to make changes might result in grave danger to my personal and spiritual development.

My understanding of the dream met all the criteria of an accurate interpretation, but I still needed to find a way to translate this new understanding into practical, waking terms. I began by reviewing the scene I had redreamed in response to item #13. The first thing I had considered was to keep the flower as a houseplant. That might have translated into physical terms as a small alteration such as staying in Miami but making a job change or department transfer. Yet I knew in my heart that it wasn't enough. Just as the flower would have still been a "kept" plant, I would have still felt like a "kept" man. Then I had realized that what the flower really needed was a total change of environment. The solution that had felt best was to transplant it to a more natural environment where it could be relatively self-sustaining and its needs met with minimal effort.

My wife and I had occasionally talked about finding an affordable home on an acre or two of land where we could have a garden. We fantasized returning to a more natural lifestyle than what we had in Miami and possibly even starting a freelance business that would make us more self-sufficient. Yet we had no idea where to go or how we could do it. The idea of just packing up and taking off inevitably brought all my insecurities bubbling up to the surface, so it had never become more than a fantasy.

But the dream changed things. Every time my thoughts went back to it, the power of its simple image compelled me to make some kind of effort to save the flower. And the haunting feeling that something very precious to me would be lost if I *didn't* act made me wonder how stable my existing situation really was. Although I wanted to take immediate action in response to the dream, relocating a family and finding new employment is not the kind of decision that is made overnight. I decided to begin by actively investigating my options. The dream-based action I took was to write a letter to a friend who was living in another part of the state and ask about housing and employment opportunities. Even that simple act was extremely satisfying for I had taken the first small step toward the resolution of my dream.

About two months later, acting more on faith in my dreams than actual employment options, I left the stifling security of my existing job to learn to survive on my own. Even during the difficult times that followed it was a decision I never regretted. Especially after I heard through a friend that the company I had worked for in Miami had gone out of business a few months after I left! Within a year, I had established a small freelance business and found an affordable home for sale in the Central Florida area with about an acre and a half of land. As my wife and I walked around the property with the owners, we learned that they were avid gardeners. They had cultivated a variety of beautiful exotic flowers (very similar to the one in my dream) that bloomed perennially in sheltered beds throughout the yard. After confirming that the dream insights also made practical sense, we bought the house.

Obviously, not all dream-based actions will be as dramatic as relocating or changing careers. More often they will involve communicating honest feelings in relationships, reassessing priorities, checking out the feasibility of dream suggestions and then taking some small symbolic step toward a new life pattern. However small the gesture, once you feel you have reached a reasonable balance between dream insights and practical considerations, make your decision and ACT. Your waking actions are the link that connects the benefits of dream insight to your daily existence.

Chapter 8

Dream Interviews

Now that we have gone through a sample dream in detail, I'd like to present a few instances of the Guided Interview approach in practice. The first entry is an example of how I typically work with dreams in my personal dream journal. Following that is an interview that demonstrates how the approach can be used with someone who is unfamiliar not only with this method, but with dreamwork in general. In the third illustration, the dreamer was very familiar with the Guided Interview approach and had been consulting her dreams for several years.

As you read these examples, you are likely to experience feelings of your own arising within you. Because of the richness of dream imagery, it is difficult to hear an account of a dream without having some kind of sympathetic emotional reaction. You may even come up with an interpretation that diverges drastically from the dreamer's own associations. Granted, it is true that a dream may have levels of meaning other than the one addressed by the dreamer. It is also true that a dreamer will sometimes resist acknowledging valid insights into a dream. But it is essential to keep foremost in mind that dreams come to the dreamer and no one else. Therefore, it is the dreamer alone who can know for certain whether or not an association "fits." The rest of us can only imagine what it might have meant if we were to have had it. While our projections might sometimes have meaningful relevance to the dreamer, they are more likely to be reflecting aspects of our own life situations.

The following dream came to me after I had been riding out the ups and down of freelance work for about three years.

Bugs Bunny Joined Survivalists

I'm an observer, watching a small band of men in camouflage clothing struggle to make their way across a searing desert. They appear to be engaged in some sort of survival exercise. Then I notice that the leader of the expedition is an eight-year-old version of myself. "Billy," as I'll call him, is taking the journey very seriously. He prides himself on being able to survive in a hostile environment against formidable odds. Even grown men can barely endure the difficulties Billy is withstanding.

The group painfully makes its way over the crest of a sand dune and stops to rest on the other side. Just then, Bugs Bunny comes casually walking up carrying a beach umbrella and a picnic basket. Stunned, Billy asks, "What are you doing here?" Bugs replies, "I heard you fellas were going on an outing, and I thought I'd join you!"

Bugs begins to set his lounge chair up under the umbrella and make himself comfortable while the others look on in amazement. Then Billy regains his composure and his hard edge. "Sure, you can join us," he says, and adds sarcastically, "I'm sure you'll have a wonderful time." But the smirk leaves his face as he watches Bugs open the picnic basket. In it are little capsules that are dehydrated and inflatable versions of everything Bugs could ever possibly want or need. He even has pockets full of what he calls "Rain Drops." They look like teardrop-shaped candies and have the word "rain" printed on them. Whenever Bugs is feeling a little hot or dry, he throws one into the air and it comes down as a small, refreshing rainshower. For Bugs Bunny, the whole thing is a picnic, and his attitude is starting to become contagious.

After recording the dream in my journal, I went through the worksheet and noted the following associations:

1) SCERC OUTLINE:

Setting	The desert in the heat of the midday sun, with nothing but sand as far as the eye can see in every direction
Characters	8-year-old Billy, Bugs Bunny, the other survivalists, and myself as an observer
Event	Billy and the survivalists encounter Bugs Bunny during a difficult desert crossing
Response	Billy reacts with sarcasm, assuming that Bugs Bunny won't stand a chance of survival in the harsh environment
Conclusion	Bugs Bunny turns out to be better prepared than anyone else to survive hardship

2) FEELING AT THE CONCLUSION:

horror fear frustration neutrality satisfaction happiness elation

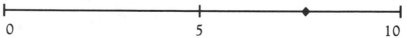

(Warning)   (Evaluation)   (Guidance)

3) VIVIDNESS/INTENSITY:

0   5   10

4) TITLE: Bugs Bunny Joined Survivalists

5) AVOIDANCE: (Avoidance was not an issue in this dream)

6) CHOICE/POLARITIES: The polarities in this dream drew attention to the disparity between Bugs Bunny's "Abundance" and Billy and the survivalists' "Need"

7) OUTSTANDING IMAGES:

Desert = Dry, harsh and inhospitable. A difficult place to survive. Reminds me of my current financial and emotional "dry spell"

Survivalists = People who pit themselves against seemingly impossible odds to prove they can endure anything. They're usually deadly serious, like I've been lately

Bugs Bunny = Humor, optimism and unshakable confidence. The way I feel when I'm clear about what I want

Dehydrated/inflatable capsules = These remind me of my own needs and desires that have recently seemed so unattainable yet have always come easily when I'm enjoying my life

"Rain Drops" = Teardrop-shaped, personal rainshowers that make you feel better when you've been having a difficult time. These remind me of how refreshing it feels to allow myself to cry sometimes when things are really rough

8) PARTICIPANTS AND MOTTOS:
Billy and the survivalists = "It takes toughness, sacrifice, and strength of will to endure the hardships of this world."
Bugs Bunny = "You fellas can struggle if you want to. For me, life is a picnic!"

9) MOST HIGHLY-CHARGED SCENE: The emotional climax was when Bugs Bunny began to set up his little beach cabana in the middle of the desert

10) I FEEL: Amazement, humility, and admiration. I'm in awe of Bugs Bunny's ability to enjoy life with all its hardships

11) I'VE HAD SIMILAR FEELINGS WHEN: I see my young sons run up to play with me after I've had a particularly rough day

12) PREDREAM CONCERNS: The past several weeks have been extremely difficult in terms of both business and personal relationships. Survival by freelancing has been a struggle and I'm not sure where to go from here

13) REDREAM/PARADREAM: If I were to have this dream again tonight, I would relinquish my leadership of the survivalists to

Bugs Bunny. He, without question, is better suited to lead us all across the desert.

14) **TRANSLATION INTO ACTION:** The solution to the dream would have been to make Bugs Bunny the leader of the expedition. In waking terms, that might mean I should stop taking my difficulties so deadly seriously and get back in touch with the humor, optimism, and confidence within me. Instead of relying on toughness and strength of will, maybe I should start relaxing and having a little fun. It also might be a good idea to redefine my goals and clarify what I really want. This dream helps me to see that the Spartan attitudes I've adopted in response to demanding situations are not nearly as effective as a well grounded sense of humor. It also suggests that all my wants and needs will be easily met as I learn to take my problems more lightly. I will act on this dream by taking my sons to Disney World this weekend instead of working as I had planned. I will also clarify my desires by listing three specific things I want to accomplish.

Because of this dream, I began taking a more lighthearted approach to the challenges with which I was faced. New opportunities suddenly started to open up. One of them was the offer of a full-time counseling position, which I decided to accept.

The next dream was shared with me while I was working as a youth counselor at a runaway shelter in Florida. A sixteen-year-old girl, whom I will call Lisa, had recently run away from her parents' home in New York. She told me she had the dream "a whole bunch of times" during the past three or four years. The most recent occurrence had been just a few days before she left New York in a car with some friends. She had been in Florida less than a week.

Lisa and I sat outside on the lawn by the swimming pool, far enough away from the other residents to afford a degree of privacy. Her clothes were stylishly casual: an oversized knit sweater, jeans, and designer tennis shoes. Our time was somewhat limited by scheduled activities, leaving us about an hour to work with the dream. Lisa told me she had never before given much thought to dreams but was very curious about this one because of its repetition and intensity. She said it had always bothered her, but had recently become so disturbing that she was afraid to get into a car. She confided feeling that it was "some kind of a warning," though she had no clear idea how it might relate to her situation. Lisa needed no encouragement to share her dream. I told her only that I was willing to listen and would help her to understand it if I could. Although I did not use an actual worksheet while we discussed Lisa's dream, I mentally followed the Guided Interview process.

LISA: *I was riding with my father in a long, white limousine. He was driving and I was sitting next to him on the passenger's side. We were coming to an intersection where you had to make a turn. I wanted to go left and told my father so, but he turned right without paying any attention to me at all. It made me furious, but he didn't even notice. He just kept on driving. After we had gone a little ways down the road to the right, we came to a place where there were dead people and coffins all around. It wasn't exactly a scary place, but it felt horrible just because everything there was dead. That's all I remember.*

WILL: Now just let me make sure I understand your dream. You and your father are in his limousine. He is driving and you are sitting next to him. Then you come to a point where you have to turn, and you and your father want to go in different directions. You tell him you want to go left, but he ignores you and turns right. Is that right so far? (Whenever I repeat a dream, I do so in the present tense. This helps the dreamer to respond from direct feelings rather than from memory.)

L: Yeah. (At this point, Lisa had confirmed the setting, characters and main event of the dream.)

W: And you respond to being ignored by your father by becoming furious, but he doesn't notice and turns right anyway. Then you come to the cemetery, right?

L: Right, except it isn't a cemetery. It's just a place with dead people and coffins. (Here, Lisa confirmed her response and corrected my mistaken impression about the conclusion. This is a good example of the importance of staying with the dreamer's own words.)

W: So how do you feel right at the end of the dream, just before you wake up?

L: I feel kind of like a zombie. Everybody feels like zombies. Just dead. I don't feel anything—just dead. (Here again, I was reminded not to assume anything about someone else's dream. Although Lisa was admittedly disturbed by the dream, she repeatedly said that it was not particularly frightening. In fact, what seemed to bother her the most was that there were no feelings at all at the conclusion.)

W: Compared with other dreams you've had, how intense would you say this one was—say, for example, on a scale of one to ten?

L: Definitely a ten. (This comment attuned me to the fact that Lisa's dream was reflecting an extremely ripe issue in her life.)

W: Can you give this dream a short title?

L: *My Father Won't Listen To Me.*

W: I sense a lot of feeling in that title. Is your father really like that?

L: Definitely.

W: Is there anything specific in the dream that you are trying to avoid?

L: Just the dead people.

W: And why is it important to avoid them?

L: Because I don't want to end up like them! The thing about this dream is that I've had it so many times that I'm afraid it's a prediction that I'm going to be killed in a car crash.

W: Dreams can be really frightening. Fortunately, my experience has shown me that dreams are more likely to reflect current emotional situations than to predict future physical ones. Maybe if we can understand the dream, it will ease your fears about it being a premonition. Do you want to go on?

L: Okay. Yeah.

W: Most dreams are built around some kind of a choice. Sometimes the choice is really obvious, but other times you need to poke around a little bit to turn it up. Do you have any sense of what choice this dream might have been built around?

L: Well, I have something important to say, and the choice might be whether or not my father is going to listen.... Maybe you could call it a choice between "new ideas" and "closed-mindedness".

W: Your father obviously plays a big part in this dream. Tell me what he's like.

L: I'm Jewish, and my family is real close and traditional. My parents expect me to attend every single family event and I don't always want to. I mean, I like my grandparents and don't mind going to some of the family gatherings. But my father expects me to spend my whole life hanging out with old people. He just doesn't seem to understand that I have my own life and my own friends. And my values aren't the same as my parents'. Having a nice big house and an expensive car and clothes is really important to them. They want me to be with people who have all those things. But I want to have friends that are just my friends.

W: So you feel like your father is trying to impose his lifestyle on you?

L: Definitely.

W: Besides your father, what other elements of this dream especially stand out?

L: Well, I remember the white limousine.

W: Tell me about the white limousine. What is it like?

L: We actually have a car like that. It's my father's. It's comfortable, expensive—like my father's lifestyle.

W: So you and your father are riding in the white limousine, and then you come to a fork in the road....

L: Not a fork. More like a "T" intersection.

W: Pretend for a minute that I know nothing about highways. What is the difference between a fork and a "T" intersection?

L: Well, a fork is where there are two directions you can go in, but they're not all that far apart. A "T" intersection is when you have two directions that are completely opposite each other... oh! (Lisa's quiet "oh" alerted me that she had made some kind of mental connection. Previous experience has taught me to attend to these clues by asking for further information.)

W: Does that remind you of something?

L: Yeah. My mom would be more like a fork in the road. We're not all that far apart. But my dad is like a "T" intersection— we just have totally opposite destinations in mind.

W: Are there any other images that come to mind?

L: Yeah, the coffins and the dead people.

W: How about giving me three words or phrases to describe them?

L: Zombie-like, no feelings, the way I feel around my father's friends... huh....

W: Something?

L: Yeah, my father's friends are like the dead people.

W: So they're the ones you don't want to be like?

L: Yeah.

W: Okay. Anything else?

L: Not really.

W: Anything about left and right?

L: Not really.

W: I'm going to ask you to give me a motto for each main character in this dream. By "motto" I mean a statement that reflects the basic viewpoint of that character. For example, Count Dracula's motto might be, "I live on the blood of others." Pollyanna's motto might be, "Always look on the bright side." Can you think of a motto for your father in this dream?

L: I guess his motto would be something like: "I don't care what you think. I'm driving."

W: Okay. And what about a motto for yourself, again, in this specific dream? Obviously, you will have different mottos in different situations.

L: "If you won't listen to me, I'm leaving." (At this point we were at item number nine on the Guided Interview worksheet, although Lisa was not aware of that. Since we were outdoors and had no drawing materials available, I asked her simply to describe to me in detail the single most highly-charged scene in the dream.)

W: Imagine this dream was a motion picture. Choose the most intense moment of the film and freeze that one frame. What would I see in that one frozen moment?

L: The most intense moment was when I was screaming at my father as loud as I could and he wasn't even looking at me. (Again, she surprised me. I had expected her to describe seeing the dead people.)

W: Okay. Now, project yourself into the scene you just described and give me at least three words that express what you are feeling.

L: *Really* frustrated, furious, helpless. I want him to listen to me! To take the things I say seriously!

W: Do those feelings pretty much describe your relationship with your father in waking life?

L: Yeah. Exactly. He never takes anything I say seriously.

W: You said the last time you had this dream was just before you left to come to Florida. Would I be safe in assuming that this issue with your father was also on your mind then?

L: Yeah.

W: All right. Imagine that you were to have this same dream again tonight, but that you are aware of the things we've talked about. What would you change about the dream? Is there anything you might do differently?

L: I'd just like to get out of the car. But I couldn't since it was moving.

W: Okay, then. Project yourself into the moving car and tell me what you are thinking.

L: I'm thinking, "I've got to get out of here, but if I jump, I might get killed."

W: Is there any way you could get out of the car without getting killed?

L: (excitedly) Maybe I could wait until he stops for gas!

W: Sounds feasible. What happens when you do that?

L: He's going to follow me. I'd better pretend I'm going to the bath-room and then sneak out and call one of my friends to come and get me.

W: And what happens when your father discovers you're missing?

L: Maybe he'll realize I really mean what I say and he'll start taking me seriously.

W: Does all this remind you of anything?

L: (laughs) Yeah. That's what I've already done! I got a ride with my friends down to Florida and I know my dad is really worried about me. But it isn't like I never want to go home again. I just want my father to understand that I have a right to spend time with my own friends and live by my own values.

W: It sort of sounds like you've already acted on this dream.

L: Yeah, I guess so.

W: Are you still worried about it being a premonition?

L: No, I understand what it's all about now. Nobody can make me join the dead people. I can make my own choices about it.

The most immediate effect of working with Lisa's dream was that her fear of riding in a car vanished. She also expressed a sense of satis-faction in knowing that she had acted on her dream even before she consciously understood it. She added, however, that working with the dream had helped her to better understand the reasons behind her running away, and why it had become necessary.

Through her work with the dream, Lisa saw that leaving her par-ents' home was never meant to be a solution. Rather, it had been a statement. With that in mind, she agreed to cooperate in making transportation arrangements back to New York. Her parents were delighted to hear of her willingness to return home, and arranged to have a ticket waiting for her at the airline counter. She flew back to New York the following day.

I did not hear from her again, and suspect there would have been many more confrontations between Lisa and her father before they were able to resolve their differences. Yet in the span of an hour, a frightening dream that had haunted her for over three years had been transformed. It had become a testament to her determination to make her needs known to her parents.

When acting as a dream guide for someone else, you will often be tempted to project your own associations onto the dream. As a rule, it is best not to venture too far into the dreamer's territory. In Lisa's dream, for example, I was intrigued by the idea that Lisa wanted to turn left and her father insisted on turning right. I was thinking in political terms; Left and Right as representing liberal and conservative thought. It made perfect sense to me that Lisa's staunchly conservative, traditional father wanted to go to the extreme right and Lisa herself, perhaps identifying with typically liberal teenage values, wanted to pursue the extreme left. I was able to control my impulses to a certain extent and refrained from throwing it right out at her. Yet I couldn't resist at least asking, "Anything about left and right?" When she didn't resonate to the suggestion, I left it alone.

I cannot overemphasize the need to resist the urge to tell a dreamer what you think their dream means. From experience, I can say that such projected interpretations are almost always either partially or completely inaccurate. Even if your interpretation should happen to be one hundred percent correct, the dreamer still tends to feel invaded and "ripped off". It is always best to remain in the role of a guide or helper (as opposed to an authority) and draw the dream's meaning out through sensitive questioning. Every human being deserves to be granted the space for self-discovery.

The next example was shared with me by my wife, Maggie. Our sons, Noah and Gabe, were nine and eleven years old at the time and becoming increasingly independent. Maggie decided to invest some of her new-found spare time working morning to mid-afternoons in an interior design outlet while the boys were in school. A few months after she had been working there, two of the three other saleswomen unexpectedly announced they were leaving the firm to take jobs with other companies. Maggie's employer called a meeting, during which she offered Maggie a position of greater authority and responsibility.

Because she hadn't been looking for full time employment, Maggie had mixed feelings about accepting the offer. She asked for a day to think it over.

Maggie and I discussed her situation and options after work that evening. At bedtime, I suggested she request guidance from her dreams on the matter. Having previously received many helpful dream insights, Maggie readily agreed. The following dream came to her that night. She told it to me the next day as we hiked along the dirt roads behind our house.

WILL: So Maggie, what's this dream you had last night?

MAGGIE: It was amazing. It was a really neat dream. *I went to visit my old college roommate, Kate. Somehow while I was with her, I learned that Gabe and Noah were not really my biological sons. Kate had raised my real sons, whom I had never met. I asked her if they were nice kids. She said, "Yes, almost as nice as Gabe and Noah." I had a deep ache, a longing to raise my own true children. I wanted to be with them, to get to know them. Kate and I went out to her back yard where my real sons were playing. I stood near the house watching them play. One was a Gemini, like Noah. I could tell by the way he acted; so carefree and happy. The older boy was an Aries, a go-getter. He looked sort of like Gabe and was about the same age, but was more like Gabe at his most bold and adventurous moments.*

W: Want to work with it?

M: You bet! I have no idea what it's saying, but I have a feeling it has to do with the job situation I asked about.

W: Okay. Do you have any initial impressions?

M: Well, I feel like it has something to do with the idea of taking on more responsibility. Maybe the dream is telling me I need to spend more time with Gabe and Noah.

W: Okay, fine. Let's set that off to the side for the moment and see what comes up as we go through the worksheet. Now the dream is set at Kate's house, and the main characters are: yourself, Kate, and your two 'real' sons who you've never before met. Is that right? (Maggie's familiarity with the Guided Interview approach enabled her to know at all times where we were in respect to the worksheet.)

M: Right. Kate and I are standing just outside her back door, watching the two boys playing in the yard. Also, Gabe and Noah aren't actually in the dream, but they are sort of implied in the background.

W: And the main event is...?

M: I find out that Kate has been raising my two real sons, that I didn't even know I had.

W: So how do you respond to this discovery?

M: I tell her I want to meet them.

W: And what is the last thing you remember happening in the dream? (Here, I'm trying to determine the dream's conclusion.)

M: Kate and I are standing out back behind her house watching my real sons playing. I'm realizing what neat kids they are and I'm looking forward to getting to know them.

W: Right at this point, just before you wake up, what are you feeling?

M: It's a good feeling; sort of an excited anticipation at the prospect of getting to know them. I'd plot it up somewhere on the right end of the worksheet scale. It feels like a guidance dream.

W: How about rating the dream's overall vividness on a scale of one to ten?

M: Pretty strong—I'd say about a seven.

W: What kind of a title could you give this dream?

M: *Getting To Know My Real Sons*.

W: Was there a sense of avoidance anywhere in the dream?

M: No.

W: What would you say could be considered the primary choice, or the polarities of this dream?

M: That's always a hard one. I'm not really sure. Do you have any ideas or feelings about it? (Occasionally, when serving as a dream guide, I am asked to suggest a starting point. I am willing to do this as long as the dreamer realizes that my projections are simply serving to prime their pump.)

W: Well, if it were my dream, I imagine I would feel pretty incredulous if someone told me my sons weren't really mine. I probably would question their claim that the other boys were my real sons. For me, the choice might have to do with whether or not I believed what I'd been told... maybe "honesty" versus "deception".

M: No, I never doubted what Kate had told me was true. As soon as I saw the two boys, I knew they were mine. The only question was whether or not I would get to know them. Oh! Now I know what the choice would be: I could either get to know them or remain a stranger.

W: Let's look at some of the outstanding images in the dream. Who is Kate, and what is she like?

M: She was my roommate and best friend during my first two years of college, though I haven't heard from her in about ten or twelve years. She is precise, organized, good with figures—all the skills I really need at work.

W: What about your two newly discovered "real sons"—what were they like?

M: They were both real energetic. The younger one seemed incredibly carefree and happy. Just as I was about to guess his sign, Kate told me he was a Gemini. I had known it by the way he acted. I asked her when the other boy's birthday was. She said it was in April, and in the dream that made him an Aries.

W: What does it mean to be an Aries? What kind of characteristics would you expect to find in an Aries?

M: I think of Aries people as being real go-getters. And like I said, the main thing I noticed about the boys was their abundance of energy. They were real rosy cheeked and constantly running around the back yard. They were playing with paper airplanes— throwing them back and forth and snatching them right out of the air.

W: Are there any other images you would like to discuss?

M: No, not really. (Actually, we could have gone on to explore Maggie's associations with a back yard as opposed to a front, the paper airplanes, or any of the other details. She seemed to want to move ahead, though, so I jotted some of the unexplored images on a notepad in case we wanted to go back to them later.)

W: Now, would you like to project yourself into each of the main characters and see what their mottos might be?

M: Well, I already know what mine would be: "I REALLY want to get to know these boys and take care of them."

W: Okay, and what about Kate; what does she have to say?

M: She says, "Well, come on out and meet them. They're right out in back."

W: How about the younger boy; what is his motto?

M: "Yeah, I'm having FUN!"

W: And the older boy... ?

M: He's ready to go! He says, "Come on, let's play ball!"

W: (Since we were hiking while working with the dream, sketching was again not an option.) Describe for me the most emotionally highly-charged scene, as if this dream were a movie and you could freeze a single frame.

M: Let's see.... I'm with Kate in her house. She has just told me that Gabe and Noah aren't my biological sons and that, unknown to me, she has been raising my real sons.

W: Project yourself into that frozen moment in Kate's house and tell me what kinds of feelings are going through you.

M: I'm amazed. I feel a powerful attraction and longing to get to know my true sons. I want to go out back and meet them!

W: So in the dream you feel "amazement, attraction, and longing" at the moment Kate tells you about your real sons. Do you recall any times in your life when you've had these same feelings?

M: Well, that's sort of how I felt when I first started looking for a job I would really enjoy... when I considered the possibility of getting paid for doing something I like.

W: You have already told me about the opportunity at work that has been on your mind since yesterday. Are you aware of any other concerns?

M: Well, I've also been wondering how it would work out with Gabe and Noah if I start working more hours.

W: That was one of the first things you mentioned when we began working with the dream; spending more time with Gabe and Noah. Let's take a closer look at that. Were you concerned in the dream about Gabe and Noah?

M: No, I wasn't. In the dream itself, I felt like my friendship with Gabe and Noah was pretty well established. There was no fear of that changing. It was the *other* sons, the ones that had been mine all along without my knowing it, that I longed to get to know.

W: Exactly what kind of a bond did you have with these two "new" sons, since you had never even been aware of their existence?

M: Well, we had a spiritual connection, a biological connection and a shared heritage. Even though I had never known about them, they were still a part of me.

W: Let me sum up what I understand of what you have told me so far. You have already established a strong friendship with Gabe and Noah that you have no fear of losing. Now you are unexpectedly presented with an opportunity to get to know new parts of yourself you never before knew existed. Does that pretty much reflect the situation?

M: Yes....

W: Does that remind you of anything?

M: Well, yes... but now I'm confused.

W: How so?

M: My first thoughts about the dream were that maybe it meant I should turn down the offer at work so I could spend more time with Gabe and Noah. But now I have the feeling that everything is fine between them and me and there are other parts of myself I'm longing to get to know. Maybe the chance to get to know them in the dream represents the opportunity that has been presented to me at work.

W: Consider this: if you did decide to accept the opportunity you've been offered at work, what kind of characteristics do you think it might bring out of you?

M: (smiling) All the characteristics of the little boys in the dream; energetic enthusiasm, bold adventurousness.... I don't know about the carefree part, though. But I would definitely get to know parts of myself I've never had a chance to explore while being a housewife for the past ten years.

W: It sounds to me like you have some pretty strong associations with the dream right now. Do you have any idea why you might have had such a different feeling about the dream before we began working with it?

M: Maybe I *wanted* to look at the dream that way because part of me is scared to take on the extra responsibilities the new position will require. I think I sort of wanted the dream to be saying that I should-n't accept the offer.

W: So how do you feel about it now?

M: I think I might really get a lot out of it. I think that, like in the dream, it would give me an opportunity to get to know parts of myself I have never before had a chance to get to know. Actually, I think it might be kind of fun, once I get used to it!

A few hours after we had returned home from our hike, the mail arrived. In it was a letter from Maggie's college roommate, Kate, who had played a leading role in Maggie's dream the previous night. Except for an occasional Christmas card, it had been more than ten years since Maggie had heard from her. In addition to news of family and friends, Kate mentioned that since she had last seen Maggie she had gotten a degree in interior design. Kate went on to explain how she had started out working with a friend, and by taking advantage of opportunities that had been presented to her, had opened up a cre-ative and rewarding business of her own.

Maggie was powerfully affected by both the dream of "longing to meet her true sons" and by the synchronicity of receiving Kate's letter immediately afterward. Before working with the dream, she had been aware of only the part of her that was afraid of the unknown. The dream put her in touch with her bold, adventurous, and energetic aspects. She chose to translate her understanding into waking action by accepting the job offer. As her dream foreshadowed, she began to develop talents that had previously only lain latent within her. By acting on that one dream, many new opportunities began to open up to her and ultimately reaffirmed her feeling of being intricately connected with all of Creation.

As illustrated by the three examples in this chapter, the Guided Interview Worksheet can be used effectively alone or with a partner, even if the partner is unfamiliar with the approach. While working with another person, however, you must continually guard against the temptation to project your interpretations onto their dream. It is for each individual to come into a personal understanding of his or her own dream. Only then can the dreamer have the sense of inner conviction necessary for making waking life changes.

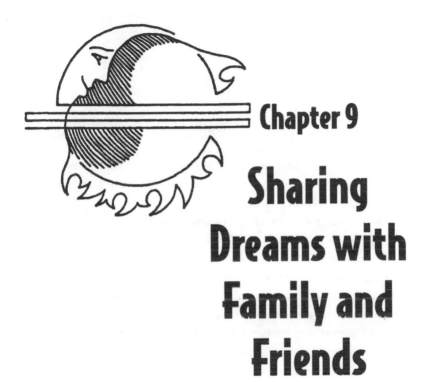

Chapter 9

Sharing Dreams with Family and Friends

Because dreams provide direct access to your own inner wisdom, it is not necessary to involve anyone else in the dreamwork process. But solo dreamwork requires a continual changing of hats. Being the interviewer one minute and the interviewee the next can distract you from being able to fully "get into" your dream. There is also the strong possibility of overlooking personal blindspots that might easily be recognized if you were going through the dream with someone who knows you well. When two dreamers work together, taking turns acting as each other's interviewer, both are freed to explore their dream in depth without interruption. Perhaps even more importantly, dreamsharing fosters a genuine intimacy rarely encountered in most relationships. For these reasons, even though you don't need to invite anyone else into your dream life, you might find you want to.

Dreams can be shared with either a partner or a small group. Both have advantages and disadvantages. A partnership generally offers more opportunity for individual participation. It's also easier to arrange a time to get together with one person than to organize a group meeting. Yet there is always the problem that you could be physically or emotionally separated from your partner when you really need to share a dream with someone. That is when the advantages of a dream group become apparent. Not only are you relatively assured of always having someone to share dreams with, but you have the additional benefits of community support and acceptance.

It is vital that everyone involved agree upon specific guidelines *before* sharing dreams with either a partner or a group. When forming a dream group, specify how many people will be participating (between four and eight is ideal; ten is probably too many). You will also need to decide how often to meet. I prefer every two weeks, although some groups meet weekly and some monthly. To get the most out of your meetings, you should also agree on the approach your group will take toward dreamwork. It's best if everyone in the group has read the same book prior to your first official meeting. If one of your members is experienced in group dreamwork, you might designate them as the group's trainer. It would then be their role to let new members know what to expect of the group and what will be expected of them.

To secure the framework of the group, guests should not be invited except on designated "Guest Nights" and any decision to include a new member should be unanimous. Also, late arrivals are a genuine problem. The focus of the group is broken and the person sharing a dream often has difficulty getting back into the mood of the dream. Plan to arrive fifteen minutes before the scheduled time. It's better to miss a meeting than to disrupt the group.

Commitment to attend regularly is essential. It may be necessary to determine how many meetings an individual can miss before he or she is no longer considered a member. If your group meets every two weeks, I suggest you require a minimum commitment of three months. Then every three months, get together not to do dreamwork, but to celebrate your friendship and assess the group's progress and needs. It's a nice touch to have the group devise some kind of simple ceremony where remaining members can renew their commitment, new members can be welcomed, and farewells can be said to those who cannot commit for the next quarter.

It is absolutely essential that any dream group or partnership be based upon a feeling of mutual trust and confidentiality. As the title of this chapter implies, dreams are not to be shared with just anybody. It should be clearly understood as well that the purpose of dreamsharing is not to analyze each other. Dream groups are a vehicle for personal growth, not therapy. Individuals with special emotional needs would be better served by a professional therapist or counselor. Dream partners or group members need to relate as equals. Your role is to serve each other first by listening and asking open-ended questions, and secondly by being available to provide additional perspectives when requested.

Occasionally, a seemingly innocuous dream image may bring up an issue that the dreamer finds embarrassing or simply prefers not to discuss. No matter how close the bond of friendship, it must be clearly stipulated that the dreamer has the authority to end the dreamwork at any point.

In addition to these general guidelines for dreamsharing, there are two special hazards of which you should be aware. The first is what I call "Trojan-Horsing." This is when someone uses a dream as the vehicle by which to gain access to another person's psyche, and then assaults them while their defenses are down. Trojan-Horsing is often unintentional, and so must be even more closely guarded against. It may even be motivated by good intentions, as in misguided attempts to subtly slip in "good advice" in the guise of dreamwork. Besides undermining the cohesion and trust upon which a dream group is built, Trojan-Horsing is simply unnecessary. If a dreamer needs correcting, his or her dreams will ultimately illuminate any errors being made.

The second, more serious, hazard might be called "dream rape." This refers to the forced and insistent projection of meaning onto someone else's dream. Those guilty of this crime may be novices but they can also be so-called "professionals" who cling to rigid dream theories. No matter what kinds of credentials an authority may possess, you, the dreamer, must ultimately judge their helpfulness. Do they help further your understanding as you go through a dream together, or do you feel invaded? Trust your feelings and never relinquish your right to final judgement of any interpretation of your dream.

Having said this, I want to make it clear that I heartily endorse the natural urge to share dreams with others. It is one of the deepest forms of intimacy a human being can ever experience. Yet, as with any kind of self-disclosure, some precautions are necessary. If the dream partners or group members are simply made aware of these potential pitfalls, they can easily be avoided or minimized. The benefits of shared intimacy, loving encouragement, and the mutual recognition of common bonds all make dreamsharing well worth the risks involved.

The next question might logically be, "Where do I find other people who are interested in sharing dreams?" Perhaps in ideal circumstances, your family would form the core of your dream group. Yet families are often bound by spirit rather than by blood. There may very well be people already existing among your circle of friends who share an unexpressed interest in dreams. Also, stay informed of continuing education classes at local colleges. People who enroll in dream classes or workshops together not only gain a common basic understanding of dreamwork, but often want to continue to meet after the course has ended. If you simply practice dreamwork on your own and stay open to new relationships, you will eventually be drawn to kindred spirits. Just be sure to keep in mind as you establish your group or partnership that for dreamwork to be effective, the dreamer must feel comfortable about sharing the dream and the interviewer must have loving intentions.

There are several qualities I have learned to associate with effective dreamworkers. One of the foremost is the ability to temporarily let go of their own personal concerns so they can give full attention to someone else's dream. This means having the self-discipline to listen without interrupting and the patience to ask, "Is there anything else?" *and wait for a response* before proceeding with another question. They can ask open-ended questions without implying they already know what the dream means and are waiting for the dreamer to catch on. When the dreamer makes a strong emotional connection, an effective dreamworker will follow rather than lead. Above all, he or she has the humility to offer a suggestion in full awareness that it may have no relevance whatsoever to the dreamer's situation.

A dream group can use the Guided Interview approach in essentially the same way it is used with a partner. When only two dreamers are involved, you might want to divide a session in half, allowing equal time for both participants. Since a group normally consists of three to eight people, there will not be time for every member to work on a dream at each meeting.

There are a number of ways to determine whose dream will be selected to work with in a group. The most obvious is to ask for a volunteer. One problem with this is that especially prolific dreamers can easily monopolize the group while meeker dreamers quietly wait to be recognized. Another way is to ask if anyone feels an especially strong need to work with their dream. Of course, this can result in a similar problem, as certain individuals are more willing than others to acknowledge their needs. A third method is to ask if anyone had an unusually powerful or vivid dream since the last meeting. This can be a good solution, as it utilizes the dreams themselves as the basis for selection. But intensity is subjective, and more than one dreamer may have had a particularly vivid dream. All things considered, I prefer to follow a "batting order" that gives whoever is up to bat the option of relegating their turn to someone else. This approach ensures that everyone will have an equal opportunity to work with a dream. It also enables the dreamer who is next in the batting order to prepare for the subsequent meeting.

A good way to begin a group meeting is to sit in silence for a minute or two while everyone gets centered. Then allow a half hour or so for the last meeting's dreamer to summarize associations or insights he or she had since then. Afterward, it's time to let the next dreamer step up to the plate.

Whenever you are relating a dream to a group, tell it in the first-person, present tense. Save any side comments for later, to avoid confusing the dream with waking events. Whenever possible, provide copies of the dream to group members so they can read along. Read the dream as expressively as possible so the other group members can vicariously experience the dream. After you have told your dream, group members may need to ask clarifying questions. This is the time for them to reflect the dream back to you in terms of the SCERC outline or clear up questions regarding specific events or images. All questions, however, should relate to the content of the dream rather than being interpretive.

Group members can take turns conducting the interview but need to resist the urge to compete with other interviewers or slip in additional questions before the dreamer has fully responded to the first.

Interviewers may want to take notes during the interview. These notes, if given to the dreamer at the end of the meeting, provide food for thought and often trigger additional insights.

As interviewers, the group members serve two primary functions. The first is to relieve you, the dreamer, of anything that prevents you from going into your dream as deeply as you want. The second is to be sensitive to your responses; recognizing when to ask questions directly from the worksheet, when to follow your tangents and when to be silent and allow your feelings to bubble up to the surface. Non-interviewing group members serve by playing the role of what I call the Cavalry. Their job is to stay abreast of what is happening during the dreamwork and come to your aid whenever you call for assistance.

Suppose, for example, the dreamwork is going well until you reach item #6, concerning the primary choice being presented in the dream. Suddenly you feel stumped. At this point you announce to the group, "I'd like some help here, please." It's extremely important that the members of a dream group all agree to refrain from offering any comments until the dreamer directly requests assistance. This helps ensure that the dreamer remains in control and is not distracted by unsolicited suggestions during the dreamwork.

In response to your request, various group members may then read you sample choices from the worksheet or make other suggestions they feel might reflect the basic polarities of the dream. You, the dreamer, decide whether or not any of their suggestions seem to fit. Someone may happen upon just the right wording. Or their suggestion may prompt you to come up with a slight variation that works perfectly. Or the entire group may be so far off in one direction that it helps you to see another more clearly.

Suppose that later in the dreamwork you find it difficult to verbalize feelings about a significant image in the dream; a mountain, for example. Here again, you would call in the Cavalry. At this point it's helpful for the dreamer to withdraw and quietly take notes while the group members close their eyes, adopt the dream as their own, and take turns describing how each of them perceives a mountain. If there are six members in your dream group, you will very likely hear six very different descriptions of a mountain. One person might say,

"My mountain is a challenge to climb. When I arrive at the top, I feel I have really accomplished something." Someone else might say, "My mountain is cold, misty, remote. I feel as though I have embarked on a solitary adventure." A third member might contribute a comment such as, "My mountain is ancient, and inhabited by wise old hermits." Yet another might volunteer, "My mountain is a ski resort in the Rockies and I'm having a wonderful time skiing and meeting new friends."

These descriptions offered by the group members reflect what a mountain might represent if it had appeared in their own dreams. The dreamer, however, may or may not resonate to those suggestions. Because of the broad base of common human experiences, associations from the group will often be personally significant to the dreamer as well. But as always, group members need to resist trying to "sell" the dreamer on any particular association.

Another point at which the group's input is often especially helpful is item #8: Participants and Mottos. Imagine you are attempting to discover the motto of one of your dream characters. You close your eyes, assume the role of that character and express a viewpoint from within that role. Let's say you sense this character has something to say to one of the others in the dream. Or perhaps there is just something about the character that intrigues you. Again, you may choose to call on the Cavalry for help. You might ask someone to play the role of the other dream character so you can engage in a dialogue. Or if you just want to examine a character's motives more deeply, you could have the group ask a series of spontaneous questions while you, still assuming the dream character's role, respond. The questions asked by the group need not be significant in themselves. You may be asked things like:

"What is your name, or what would you like to be called?"
"How do you feel about the other characters in this dream?"
"What do you see as your purpose in this dream?"
"What could the dreamer learn from you?"
"How would you like to see this dream turn out?"

Within the overall time restraints of the group meeting, always allow the dreamer to set the pace of the interview. Dream understanding unfolds according to its own timetable and should neither be hurried along nor held back by group members. Not every dream will be completely understood in the span of a single session. Yet clues and insights that surface during the group work often prove to be pivotal in the dreamer's thinking during the days that follow.

SUMMARY OF A TYPICAL DREAM GROUP MEETING

1) Begin with a moment of silence, followed by feedback from the previous meeting's dreamer.
2) Have the dreamer who is "up to bat" read their dream in first-person, present tense (preferably while the group reads along).
3) Allow group members to clarify the content of the dream (*without* interpretive comments) using the SCERC outline as an aid.
4) Have group members take turns interviewing the dreamer, using the worksheet flexibly as needed. GIVE THE DREAMER ADEQUATE TIME TO RESPOND, then repeat or summarize the dreamer's response before proceeding to the next question.
5) Any time the dreamer feels "stuck," he or she can call in the Cavalry and take notes while group members take turns adopting the dream as their own.
6) Near the end of the meeting, have either the dreamer or one of the lead interviewers summarize the connections that have been made.
7) Remember that dreams are local maps. Don't try to plot out an entire life course from a single dream.

So far I have addressed dreamwork only as it pertains to adults. Yet when discussing the topic of dreams within a biological family, children's dreams need to be considered a top priority. Young children's lack of experience in the physical world is balanced by an increased awareness of their dreams. As a result, children's dream experiences tend to weigh heavily in their overall world view.

My own two sons began sharing dream fragments with me as they began to talk, around two or three years old. Most of their early dream reports were one sentence descriptions upon awakening such as, "I dream 'bout alligator... RRrraahr!" Occasionally, I would overhear one or the other of them talking in his sleep and jot down a quick note in the dream journals I had begun keeping for each of them. I can still recall the intense curiosity I felt as I heard my three-year-old son sleepily mumbling, "... One, two, three... okay guys, let's GO!"

Sometimes their dreams apparently convinced them of the necessity of certain activities they disliked. When my youngest son was two and a half, for example, he intensely disliked having his fingernails clipped. Early one morning, after the previous evening's unsuccessful attempt to cajole him into cooperating, he told me a dream he had just had. "When I was sleepin'," he said, "my fingernails got bigger and bigger and bigger and bigger and I couldn't eat! An' I couldn't drink, either!" We laughed together at the outrageous imagery of his dream, but he never again gave me a problem when his fingernails needed to be trimmed.

One of my own earliest dream memories took place around the same young age and served an equally important function. In the naiveté of early childhood, I believed that movies were made all at once, rather than being shot in short scenes. My recurrent dream involved the making of a cowboy picture. In the dream, I would be watching the cowboy hero and wondering what would happen if he suddenly had to go to the bathroom right in the middle of the movie. At that point, the cowboy would invariably climb down from his horse, find a suitable bush or tumbleweed to hide behind and relieve himself.

The first few times I had this dream as a toddler, I failed to recognize its warning and awakened to a cold, soggy mattress. Gradually, I learned to associate the dream with its unpleasant aftereffects. The instant the cowboy swung his leg over the back of the saddle to dismount, I would wake myself up and sprint to the bathroom! Whenever I relate this experience in a dream class, it inevitably elicits blushing confessions of similar early childhood dreams from one or two of the class members. These repeated accounts suggest that it is in their dreams that young children learn nighttime bladder control.

It appears inevitable that at some point children will begin to encounter frightening dreams. One evening at bedtime when my eldest son was nearly four, he uncharacteristically turned to me and said, "I don't wanna go to bed, Dad."

"Why not, Gabe?" I asked.

"Because strange things happen when I dream."

"What kind of 'strange things'?"

"Dinosaurs."

"Dinosaurs? What else?"

"Sometimes it rains real hard and the water gets too deep and I can't keep walking." Tears began to fill his eyes and I realized he was genuinely upset.

This was one of Gabe's first really unpleasant dream experiences, and it seemed to make him a little distrustful of his dreams afterward. Although the "Dummy Dreams," as he called them, were a small minority of the dreams he shared, they caused him to become increasingly apprehensive about going to sleep when bedtime arrived. When the problem became worse instead of better during the following weeks, I decided to try to find a way to help him.

A few of the dream books I had read mentioned the possibility of dealing with frightening dream events and hostile dream characters by taking action within the dream itself. They generally advocated conquering the enemy and demanding a gift, or even fighting the enemy to the death. I was reluctant to train my son to become a four-year-old dream commando, but found the idea of teaching him to confront his fears directly within his dreams intriguing. I began to experiment with various strategies within my own dreams, looking for one I could feel comfortable teaching my sons. In the end, I settled on a sort of Gandhian "non-violent, non-cooperation with evil" approach. I advised my young sons to yell for help when threatened in their dreams, even fight to defend themselves if necessary, but stand their ground rather than running away.

Both boys accepted the suggestion as unquestioningly as they had earlier followed my instructions on tying their shoes. Unlike many adults to whom I have given similar advice, they never doubted the possibility of acting intentionally within a dream. Not long afterward, I began to notice changes in both of my sons' dreams. Gabe discovered, to his complete delight, that when he called out in his dreams, a "Fairy Queen" would appear to help him. The Fairy Queen appeared frequently as Gabe's guardian angel for the better part of a year. Although he still had occasional frightening dreams, the fearful apprehension he had displayed earlier was gone. Over the course of that year and the recording of sixteen more of his dreams, I noticed that the Fairy Queen became simply The Queen. Also, Gabe gradually began to assume the role of her protector instead of the other way around.

By the age of seven or eight, both boys seemed to have developed the habit of confronting frightening dream characters. The courage they developed in their dreams not only eased their nighttime fears, but also began to carry over as bolder attitudes in their waking lives. Their new dream skills often seemed to transform potential nightmares into dreams from which they would awaken feeling almost heroic. The following entry from Gabe's journal (as related to me) is an example of such an experience.

The Western Glob

The Western Glob (Gabe's dream, age eight)

I was with Mom in a western town in the old days. We were both wearing western clothes and were standing out in front of a saloon that had those kind of doors that swing open. We went in and had a drink. Then, all of a sudden, the other people in the room all stared toward the door and got really scared. I looked out the door, too, and saw a big globbery thing coming over a hill toward the saloon. It didn't have any shape except for a face. The rest was just a big glob. When I turned back around, Mom wasn't there anymore.

Then I remembered what you told me, Dad! I went outside and started yelling at it and waving my arms, and it just globbered away back over the hill.

In addition to learning to confront fears in dreams, it may also be possible to learn physical skills. My youngest son, Noah, wanted to learn how to ride a bicycle. Being seven, he was easily old enough, but because of the soft sand roads near our house he had never had the opportunity to try. One Friday evening after dinner, Noah arranged to borrow his brother's bicycle and asked me to drive him to a nearby subdivision that had smooth, paved streets. By the time we had loaded the bike and family in the truck, daylight was already beginning to fade. I had time to give him two good pushes that, after about twenty feet, resulted in two impressive crashes. By then it was too dark to keep on trying.

On the way back home, I recalled having read an article about an experiment that University of Chicago researchers conducted in the 1970s. Students who all had about the same free-throw ability in basketball were divided into three groups. The first group was instructed not to play basketball at all for thirty days. The second group was told to practice shooting free-throws one hour per day for thirty days. The third group, like the first, was told not to play basketball at all, but to *visualize* themselves shooting free-throws one hour per day for thirty days. At the end of the thirty day period, the first group, which had not practiced at all, made no improvement on their original score. The second group, which had practiced daily, improved by 24%. The third group, which had only practiced mentally, also improved their free-throw ability by an astounding 23%.

I explained my idea to Noah and asked him if he wanted to try an experiment. The movie, "Pee Wee's Big Adventure," had just opened at the movie theater. The entire movie centered on bicycles and bicycling. We went to the movie and I even had Noah draw a picture of a bicycle before he went to bed. After he had fallen asleep, I went in to check on him and gently whispered bike riding tips while he slept. The next morning, Noah shared the following brief dream.

Bike-Riding Down A Hill

Bike-Riding Down A Hill (Noah's dream, age seven)
I was riding my bike down this real long hill. The hill went down for a ways, then back up a little bit. Then it went down again, then up a little again—sort of like in steps—so I could ride really far without having to pedal all the time!

After telling me his dream, Noah was anxious to take the bike out and try again. Once more, we loaded it up and drove back to the same subdivision without even taking time for breakfast. I gave him a push, just as I had the previous evening. This time, though, one push was all he needed. He rode nonstop all the way around a large, oval-shaped drive and was even able to stop and turn under control on his way back. It could be that he had only gained a new sense of confidence. Maybe he actually developed new skills within his dream. But it is a fact that he never fell once while riding almost continually all morning.

Because of their impressionability and instinctive submission to adult authority, I feel that working symbolically with young children's dreams is usually inappropriate. Yet there is another even more important reason I rarely discuss with children the symbolism of their dreams. They are simply not interested. Let me be quick to point out, though, that this does not mean children's dreams should be disregarded or that they are less important than those of adults. It may be even more important for children to acknowledge their most memorable dreams. Dreams are, after all, a primary overflow valve for the overwhelming emotions that occur so often during childhood. This does not mean you should put stressful expectations on children to recall their dreams. Instead, I advocate the creation of an open, trusting environment in which they can feel free to share a dream without fear of ridicule or criticism.

Children are justifiably proud of anything that is their own unique production. Even a toddler's fascination with the toilet is understandable considering it's the manufacturing center for one of the few things he can create independently at that stage of life. Therefore, when a child shares a dream with you, regard it as an honor. You are being trusted with a glimpse into their private inner world. Listen attentively and non-judgmentally, regardless of the dream content. Children instinctively withdraw the tendrils of their inner life at the first sign of judgment or censorship, no matter how tactfully it is expressed.

Dream sharing, then, strengthens the family bond through the giving and receiving of trust that it requires. It may be impossible, as a dream conscious parent, to avoid projecting meaning onto your child's dream. But you can at least keep it to yourself. Dreams themselves are a healing force and will serve the child's needs without any adult's interpretive intervention.

There are ways to reinforce the beneficial influences of a child's dream that are not impositions, however. Most of the items on the Guided Interview Worksheet, when taken out of an interpretive context, are non-interpretive and perfectly appropriate for use with children. In fact, children often find them highly satisfying and a lot of fun as well.

Take item #9, for instance. Unlike adults, most young children are free of inhibitions about drawing their dreams. Prepare yourself, though, because contrary to the pervasive adult belief that childhood is a time of innocence and joy, many of your child's dreams will be disturbing. Yet when a child puts a dreamscape on paper, the scene becomes effectively frozen in time. Any monsters, boogie-men, and bad guys are placed safely at arm's length where they can be examined from a less threatening position. Once freed from the immediacy of nightmare panic, the child can consider aspects of the dream he may want to change. As a parent, you can help by encouraging him to come up with his own possible solutions to the situation.

After getting the child's emotions on paper in the original drawing, encourage him to revise it by incorporating the changes he would like to make (item #13 on the worksheet). In a sense, redrawing a disturbing dream is like a fire drill. It allows a child to rehearse responses to frightening or dangerous situations that could later prove to be of great benefit.

A drawing of a favorite dream, on the other hand, can help a child to visualize and remember the scene more clearly. This kind of drawing can become a visual affirmation of the child's fondest hopes. Simply by viewing the picture, he can to some extent reexperience the joy embodied in the dream while focusing on what he wants to create in his life.

Naturally, drawing is only one form of an endless scope of noninterpretive dreamwork. Any medium can be used to express the dream, from collage to sculpture to mask making. Another form of dream expression popular with children is role playing, or Dream Theater, as it is sometimes called. After relating a dream, the child/director casts available family and friends in appropriate roles. Taking their cues from the young dreamer, the participants act out the dream. Hostile dream characters tend to lose their hard edge and become much more approachable when portrayed by trusted companions. While some dreams lend themselves to Dream Theater productions more readily than others, all dreams have certain aspects that can be creatively reenacted. Noah's bike riding dream, presented earlier in the chapter, is one illustration of a simple reenactment.

In the same way that dream sharing can benefit parent-child relations or strengthen the bond between friends, so it also can reinforce intimacy within a marriage. It is never more important than in a committed relationship to understand another person's point of view. Because of the depth of feelings and intertwining of lives in a marriage, emotional boundaries tend to blur. As a result, partners often become entangled in each other's personal dilemmas. Dreams can bring our attention back to the individual origins of our difficulties and show us how we are contributing to our own problems. This helps to break the cycle of blame and defensiveness and allows both partners to view each other's situation with greater compassion. In sharing dreams, we are laying all our cards on the table. This sharing of personal fears and fantasies, trials and triumphs, leads to a deep mutual understanding and empathy. The acknowledgment and acceptance of the diverse characters in our dreams also makes us less inclined to be judgmental of others in waking life.

My wife, Maggie, and I have developed a dream sharing tradition that helps to maintain closeness in our marriage. About once a week on the average, we make a date to go on what we call our "dreamhike." During this time, we exercise body and soul by doing dreamwork together while hiking along the dirt roads near our house. Each of us has an opportunity to share a recent dream. Then we work with either one or both of them, depending on how long it takes to get a genuine feeling of satisfaction from our understanding of the dream images. Sometimes that feeling comes simply in the telling of the dream. Other dreams may take much longer.

We tend to take a playful approach to our dreams, no matter what the content, and use the worksheet flexibly. We may be discussing a dream image and go so far off on a tangent that we both forget even having started out with a dream. Ironically, it is often just at that point that one of us will make a casual comment that suddenly snaps us back to the dream and lays the imagery wide open. There is an incredible sense of spontaneity and joy that accompanies the understanding of a dream. It is a feeling, shared by dreamer and dream partner alike, of participating in something both universal and infinitely personal.

Because emotional "weather," like its external counterpart, is in constant flux, there will inevitably be times of marital turbulence. During these periods, there is a natural inclination to withdraw the trust that makes dream sharing possible. When a couple has developed a tradition of mutual dreamwork, the loss of closeness is particularly noticeable and painful. Like physical touch or sexual intimacy, dream sharing often becomes such a pleasantly anticipated form of affection that the very lack of it can be a strong motivation to reunite. On other occasions, a dream may inspire a reunion by more direct means, as was the case with the following entry from my journals.

Maggie and I had been communicating only minimally for several days following an argument. During this time, it seemed we were confronted with one crisis after another. The bank turned down a loan I had been counting on; someone broke into Maggie's car and stole her purse; a major setback arose just before the deadline of a project I was completing, and our family cat was hit by a car and seriously injured. Then I had the following dream:

Unite For Common Survival

I'm living in a medieval forest settlement. All the villagers, myself included, are completely absorbed in squabbles and petty concerns. Then, while on an errand near the outskirts of town, I learn that there are several marauding giants heading in our direction. I race back to the village and pound on door after door, shouting, "Stop your squabbling! There's no time to indulge in these kinds of trivial distractions! We need to unite for our common survival!"

I awakened with the urgent message still on my lips. As soon as I had readjusted to physical consciousness, I reflected back on the dream and felt an instantaneous comprehension of its meaning. The dream was saying to me the same thing I had been saying to the villagers: "Listen to me! There are great dangers afoot and you're wasting time feuding. You have more important matters to attend to right now!" I immediately went to Maggie and shared the dream just as it had occurred, without interpretation. She, too, instantly recognized the validity of its reflection and we both took steps to begin reestablishing communication and cooperation.

In instances such as the above example, where dreams are shared during periods of emotional separation or early stages of reconciliation, I recommend that special precautions be taken. Because of lingering ill feelings, the dangers of Trojan-Horsing and dream rape are greater than normal. Instead of attempting to work symbolically with the dream images, I suggest you share only the dreams themselves exactly as they occurred. The trust that is essential for effective dreamwork cannot be called up at will. And just the sharing of dreams themselves can often communicate your deepest feelings where words have failed.

The healing tendencies of acknowledged dreams may not guarantee the resolution of waking conflicts, but they seem to encourage movement in that direction. As with any other form of shared dreamwork, though, basic guidelines must be agreed upon and respected when sharing dreams with a mate. And no matter how strong your marriage or friendship, I recommend you do not trade dream journals with each other. It's too easy to start unintentionally censoring your dreams while recording them or directing your writing toward someone other than yourself. Read your dreams to each other, share as much as you feel is comfortable, but keep your journals private. They should be the one place in the world where you are free to be totally honest, candid, and spontaneous.

Sharing dreams with other people need not always be a serious business. In fact, a playful attitude will often prove more beneficial than an overly somber one. Playfulness opens you to a boundless array of opportunities for adventure and creativity. Dreams can be made into games and built as projects. One evening, for instance, I challenged my young sons to join me in a dream treasure hunt. We agreed that we would try to go into our dreams, find a treasure and bring it back into the physical world. It could be any kind of treasure at all; a picture, song, story, invention or whatever. As I tucked them into bed I added, "Look for something really unusual—you might even discover your special Symbol!" I was referring to the mystical designs (Jung called them mandalas) that sometimes appear in dreams. The boys knew what I meant, since they were both familiar with a Celtic cross-shaped emblem that had appeared in one of my dreams before they were born.

Early the next morning, Noah padded excitedly into the bedroom while I was jotting down my own dream. He showed me a piece of paper with an odd looking design he had carefully drawn out with a marker. Then he told me his dream:

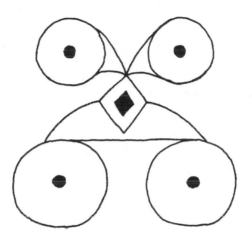

Noah's Symbol

Got My Symbol (Noah's dream, age five)

I saw a kid from my kindergarten class. He had blond hair and was wearing a red shirt and long blue pants. He had brown eyes.... I can't remember his name. It was kind of neat, because he was waiting for me. He actually knew I was going to come and so he sat at his desk and drew out the symbol for me. He already had it drawn when I got there and he just gave it to me. When I woke up, I drew what he drew. Oh yeah, his name was Matt.

After Noah and I had discussed his dream, I told him about the one I had been writing down when he had come in:

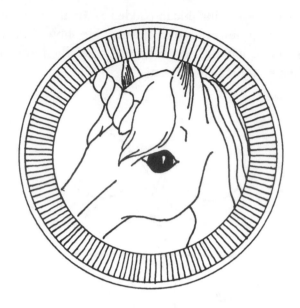

The Unicorn Patch

The Unicorn Patch

I'm in high school and remember I'm supposed to find and bring back a treasure. I want to do it right away so I don't forget, and so I can get back to my regular adventures. Bringing back the treasure feels sort of like another homework assignment, and I want to get it over with. I find it lying on a counter where someone has left it for me to pick up. It's a beautiful cloth patch, sort of like a Boy Scout merit badge, with a close-up of a blue-eyed Unicorn's head on it. The border is red and the background is white.

Gabe was sleeping in the next room and awakened to the sounds of Noah and I telling each other our dreams. When we asked if he remembered anything, Gabe replied that he could not. He expressed a little disappointment, but knew he would have many more chances. A few weeks later, the subject of personal Symbols came up again and he decided to give it another try. That night his special Symbol literally came to him.

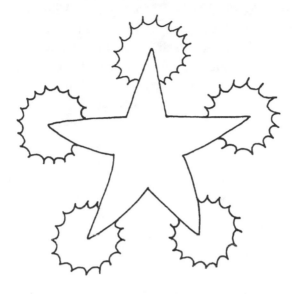

Gabe's Symbol

My Symbol Made Me Fall Out Of Bed (Gabe's dream, age seven)
   I saw my symbol 'way far off. The star was white and the cir-
cles of fire were yellow. It's easy to draw, because the top of the
star is like the head, the middle is like the arms and the bottom is
like the legs. It was coming toward me and sort of slowly turning as
it came. Then it just whirled right up at me really fast and made
me fall right out of my bed! Then I got off the floor and drew it.

With Christmas approaching, I thought it would be fun to make a
family present using the unique Symbols we had each received in our
dreams. I went to my woodshop and built four round plywood shields
with sturdy handles. Then I carefully painted our individual designs
on the shields, being certain to use the same colors that had appeared
in the dreams. The dream shields were a big hit and soon developed
into a family game.

The game is played outdoors with a small, inflatable ball. It's begun by throwing the ball up into the air. Whoever manages to catch it on the rebound then tries to tag the other players by throwing the ball at them. Each player's defense, of course, is his or her dream shield. There is a wonderful, almost magical feeling that comes with being protected by your own special symbol. Since the dream shields are all the same size (14" diameter), smaller children have the inherent advantage of being able to hide almost entirely behind their shields. We also made a "three hits and you're out" rule to regulate the length and later added an "any hits above the shoulders count against the thrower" rule for safety's sake. The last rule, for fairness, is that you can be no closer than one staff length (about 6 feet) when you throw the ball. The game developed into a family favorite. We call it "Staff and Shield."

There is no limit to the ways in which dream creativity can be used to enrich waking life. One especially rewarding project is to make a Character Collage. Go through old magazines and cut out pictures of people or animals that remind you of your most memorable dream characters. Separate them if you wish, but acknowledge both heroes and villains, for they are all members of your dream family. Another idea is to make a dream scrapbook. Include in it your favorite dream, your most frightening dream and the earliest dream you can remember from your childhood. As your collection grows, you can add other categories such as Funniest, Most Erotic, Most Disgusting or Most Helpful. You may want to include special sections in which to record precognitive dreams and dreams that occurred around the time of births, weddings, and deaths.

Dreamwork need not be lengthy and time consuming. Sometimes a dream will reveal itself clearly and poignantly when placed into a structured format such as the traditional three line, 5-7-5 syllable form of a Japanese haiku poem. The sample dream, "Flower In A Shallow Pan," for instance, might become:

> Beautiful flower
> pleading in desperation
> I'm its only hope.

You can even put your dream into comic strip form, as Noah did with one of his favorite dreams from his journal.

Diamond Caves (Noah's dream, age five)

Diamond Caves, 1st Panel

Me, Dad, Mom, Gabe, and a couple of friends are looking for someplace to make a fort when we find a cave in a big rock. We go inside and find a real diamond—not glass—about a foot long. There are also lots of little colored glowing things inside our cave. When I look really close, I see that they are diamonds, too. We just keep them there to decorate the cave.

Diamond Caves, 2nd Panel

Some other people are trying to find a cave like ours, but the one they find only has little diamonds and they're just glass. They like our cave and want to come in. They're really nice, but our cave just isn't big enough for everybody.

Diamond Caves, 3rd Panel

So they go back to their cave and find a little piece of a glowing leaf. They bring it to us and say, "Since this won't make our cave nicer than yours, we'll just put it in yours to help decorate it." We say, "No, thank you. We have enough stuff—why don't you put it in your own cave?"

Diamond Caves, 4st Panel

So they do, and suddenly their whole cave starts glowing kind of a brown color. Then it starts glowing all different colors of the rainbow. Then we find a leaf that's glowing green and blue. We put it at the top of our cave and it starts to sort of rain down all different colors of light.

That's when I woke up.

Dreams are indisputably personal in origin. But when they are shared willingly, with full respect for individual boundaries, their value is greatly enhanced. The dreamer benefits from group dreamwork by gaining access to a larger and more objective perspective. The group profits from both the dreamer's revelations and the satisfaction of knowing they have been active participants in the spiritual growth of another human being. And for everyone involved, there is the added benefit of heightened intimacy and deeper understanding between family, friends, and lovers.

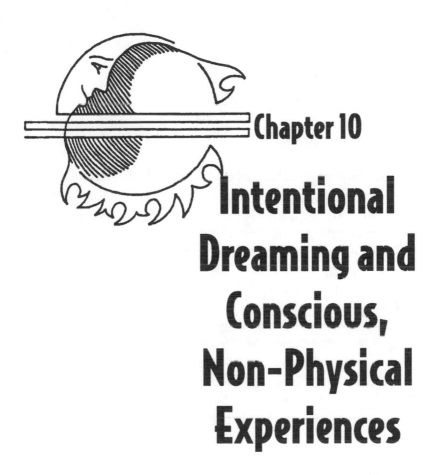

Chapter 10

Intentional Dreaming and Conscious, Non-Physical Experiences

We usually think of dreams as events over which we have little, if any, influence. They seem to happen *to* us, as opposed to being objects of our own creation. The very existence of nightmares and other unpleasant dream experiences seems to bear out this point of view. Few of us, after all, would choose disturbing dreams if we realized we had any say in the matter. Yet when you make the conscious decision to pay attention to your dreams, gradual and predictable positive changes in content inevitably appear. Perhaps a disturbing recurrent dream you worked with no longer troubles you. Or maybe since attending to your dreams, you recall more pleasant ones than you used to. These kinds of changes are evidence that conscious efforts can, indeed, influence the content of your dreams.

There are essentially two ways in which the content of a dream can be directly influenced. The first is by predream programming, or Intentional Dreaming, as I call it. Intentional dreaming means deciding *before you go to sleep* that you will direct your dreams toward a specific waking concern or perform a particular task within the dream (such as flying, for instance). The second method, commonly called Lucid Dreaming, involves changing the content of the dream *from within the dream state itself*.

Intentional Dreaming is an easily learned skill with limitless potential applications. You can use it to explore new possibilities, gain insights into specific health or relationship concerns or to just plain have fun. Sometimes called "dream incubation," this process has been used for thousands of years by civilizations throughout the world.

There are as many means of focusing one's predream thoughts as there are intentional dreamers. The methods range from simple prayer or meditation to elaborate rituals involving fasting, chanting, or sleeping in special places. The only essential requirement, however, is that you focus your thoughts clearly and succinctly. A straightforward method of doing this is simply to write down your intention or request. Compose an entire paragraph if necessary to clarify your thoughts, but then condense it into a single line. Clearly worded intentions reap clear dreams. Also, a short, meaningful statement or question is easier to repeat mentally as you fall asleep.

A dream's natural tendency is to reflect the emotional top priorities in the dreamer's personal life. But that does not mean you cannot intentionally dream about a social issue. It just means you need to raise the emotional priority of that social issue. The best way to bring any subject into your dreams, of course, is to involve yourself in it as much as possible in waking life. Study it, learn as much as you can about it, read about it and look at pictures related to it just before falling asleep.

In late 1988, for example, I volunteered to participate in a dream exchange between individuals in the United States and the Soviet Union. Both American and Soviet dreamers agreed to focus on the question, **"How can the United States and Russia work together to solve pressing global problems?"** I already had the necessary interest in the issue. That was why I had chosen to become involved in the project. My predream focusing ritual consisted of putting a globe on my nightstand and spending several minutes before going to sleep orienting myself to the relative locations of the two countries. It also helped to remind myself that Russian dreamers were making the same kinds of preparations. I went to bed at midnight with my request clearly in mind.

The following dream is one of five that I recorded that night. The first two, which I wrote down around 5:00 a.m., appeared to be addressing fairly high priority personal issues. After recording them, I briefly refocused on my intention and went back to sleep. The last three dreams occurred between 5:00 a.m. and 7:00 a.m.. The content of all three was directly related to the U.S.-Soviet question, but the one excerpted below was particularly intriguing.

Honest Communication Better Than Violence

I've just left a meeting that took place at a church. Just outside the door is a blank chalkboard sign normally used to announce church activities. I want to remember something that was said in the meeting about the Russians looking for a "resolution," not a "revolution." So I pick up a piece of chalk and write: "THE RUSSIAN RESOLUTION—HUMAN EXPERIENCE." After writing it in chalk, I step back to look for my pen and paper so I can recopy it and take it home with me.

As I'm getting out my writing materials, five or six young men pass by and see the sign. They start making angry comments about a church putting up a sign that appears to be friendly toward Russians. They start throwing stones at the sign. Some stones miss and hit the church's sliding glass door. I'm afraid they will break the glass door so I walk over to them and say, "Listen, that sign is erasable. If you don't like what it says, why don't you just erase it and write whatever you want it to say?"

The angry young men had not realized the sign could be changed. Now that they see it is, they accept my suggestion. I'm watching them gather around the sign to write something. I expect what they write won't be very complimentary, but at least it's better than throwing stones.

After awakening, I recorded my dreams and jotted down the thoughts and associations that came to mind. Essentially, I felt the dream was helping me to see that hostile, nationalistic attitudes can't be eliminated, but they can be vented in less destructive ways. The dream seemed to be promoting the idea of holding public forums. The logic was that when people are allowed to express their strongest feelings openly, their emotions are less likely to erupt into dangerous, destructive acts.

The reference to Russia in this example made it easy to recognize the connection between the dream and my predream intention. Not all intentional dreams will be so transparent. Don't be too quick to judge them as being unrelated to your request, though, for it is very possible that you are simply being distracted by the imagery of your dream. Try applying the Guided Interview worksheet and see if the underlying themes bring any connections to mind.

Intentional dreaming need not always involve a problem or question. You might choose instead to visit a friend, take a cosmic vacation, or just inject a bit of levity into your life. You are free in your dreams to do anything and go anywhere you please. If you decide to embark on this type of dream adventure, you will find it helpful to write on your notepad an appropriate affirmation. If you want to fly, for instance, you might write, "Tonight I fly!" Then as you are falling asleep, imagine yourself in every way possible either preparing for flight or actually flying.

That was exactly how the next example came about. I had awakened around 6:10 a.m. to record a dream and laid down to go back to sleep around 6:25 a.m.. Then it occurred to me that this was an ideal opportunity to do some experimentation. I closed my eyes, relaxed and began visualizing myself running laps around our large back yard in preparation to take off and fly.

Flying Near Tropical Coastline

I'm on about my fourth lap around the back yard when I suddenly feel a tearing sensation at my chest. A large knife has somehow painlessly sliced a chunk of skin off my chest, about a foot in diameter and two inches thick. It comes off in three concentric circles, like slicing the curved edge of an onion. At first I feel frightened and stop to hold the flaps of skin against my chest, thinking it has to heal. Then I realize it is no longer attached. I lay it aside, surprised to see it isn't bloody but simply moist and tender.

I start walking and feel so incredibly light and healthy that I begin to run. Normally I consider running a fairly mundane activity, but right now it feels as exhilarating as flying. That thought reminds me to try flying. I begin running along a long sidewalk beside a tropical coastline. My strides become longer and longer leaps until I'm gliding twenty or thirty feet at a time. Once airborne, I discover that clenching my fists enables me to remain in the air. Although I'm only a few feet off the ground, I can go higher by squeezing my fists. Once I reach my desired altitude I can relax my grip and continue cruising at that height.

I find my favorite altitude to be about twenty feet. I feel safe at that height and enjoy watching the ground whiz by beneath me. I have to watch out for occasional power lines, but am able to avoid them by tightening and relaxing my grip, which in turn controls my altitude. Eventually I come to a wooden bunkhouse where my wife and close friends are just putting all our kids to bed. I walk in and greet them. We all talk for awhile until, one by one, they become sleepy and go off to bed. I'm not tired and remain alone in the living room. I make myself comfortable in a rocking chair and close my eyes for a moment. When I open them again, I'm back in my physical bed and the clock on the dresser shows the time as 7:07 a.m.. The entire experience took less than forty minutes.

Although I had intended this dream simply to be an adventure, its imagery, like that of all dreams, is rich with symbolism. The three layers of skin that came off my chest, for instance, were incredibly intriguing. They brought to mind the classical descriptions of layers of increasingly ethereal bodies that exist just beneath or within the physical form. I might have wanted to consider the symbolism of a tropical coastline as well, or the unusual technique of "fist-flying." I also could have examined the relevance of the fact that I felt most comfortable flying at an altitude of about twenty feet. Or I could forget symbolism altogether and just relish the memory of the adventure. As always, it's the dreamer's choice.

The second means of directly influencing the content of a dream goes one step further. Whereas intentional dreaming takes conscious intentions to the very threshold of a dream, this approach carries those intentions past the threshold and into the dream itself. When this happens, you suddenly find yourself operating consciously within a non-physical reality.

Among sleep and dream researchers, this phenomenon is commonly called Lucid Dreaming. It is defined as "being aware you are dreaming while you are dreaming." While the term "lucidity" is popular, it is highly ambiguous since "dreaming" itself defies concise definition. Another problem in labeling dreams as either lucid or non-lucid is that very few dreams will rest contentedly in those black-or-white categories. Most would more accurately be categorized as one of infinite shades of gray. "Flying Near Tropical Coastline," for instance, could not be considered lucid by that definition, since I made no attempt within the dream to *declare* my environment a dream. Yet I entered it with full awareness, remembered my predream intention and, to a large extent, consciously selected the dream content.

Prior to my involvement with the Association for the Study of Dreams, my interests led me to become involved with many different groups that explored the nature of consciousness. In 1971, for instance, I was part of a group that had received a grant to study psychic phenomena. One of our areas of investigation involved lying down with eyes closed, relaxing, and inducing what our instructor referred to as an Out-of-Body Experience. Others with whom I studied described the non-physical realm of existence as the Astral Plane. The exploration of this plane, which took place during either meditation or sleep, was known as Astral Traveling. This term, however, was regarded with disdain by yet another group, Eckankar, in which I also participated. Eckankar practitioners insisted the Astral Plane was merely the lowest of a highly structured hierarchy of realities, and preferred the term Soul Travel to describe their inner journeys.

What these groups have in common is that they regularly deal with phenomena extending well beyond the scope of normal conversation. As a result, each has been forced out of necessity to develop and define its own terminology. Despite the syntactical disagreement, my experience in each group has convinced me that all these terms are describing various aspects of essentially the same thing. In an attempt to avoid all partisan definitions, I have come up with a generic label I use inclusively to describe these phenomena. At the risk of creating yet another term, I call them Conscious, Non-physical Experiences, or CNEs. I suspect the particulars of each CNE, by whatever name it is called, result largely from the beliefs and expectations of the individual who is having the experience.

A CNE may be intentionally induced, or it can occur spontaneously. The degree of lucidity during a CNE varies tremendously. The experience may last for quite some time, or appear only fleetingly. CNEs occur most frequently during sleep, but also may be encountered during meditation, drug-induced states, or on rare occasions even during times of physical activity. The classic Near Death Experience can be classified as a CNE as well without insinuating, against adamant denial by those who have had the experience, that their near-death encounter was some kind of dream. A CNE can be an exhilarating experience of unconditional love or it can be a terrifying confrontation with the unknown. The nature of the experience depends upon how well prepared the individual is for the event.

Admittedly, CNEs sound like feats that could only be attempted by yogis or mystics. Yet every child who has stopped wetting the bed at night has had to first master the rudiments of conscious dreaming by learning to arouse himself from sleep at a critical moment during the night. The same fundamental level of awareness is also commonly used to temporarily escape nightmares by awakening. With practice, this basic ability can be developed to the point where we can consciously choose our responses within the dream state instead of always reacting from automatic reflex. We can even choose to create new dreamscapes right in the midst of an ongoing dream.

When I first stumbled onto the idea of consciously manipulating ongoing dreams, I found it a thrilling prospect. It seemed to open doors to almost infinite possibilities. I immediately began trying to test the limits; to explore the boundaries of dream experience. Eventually, the documentation of my own journals began to confirm that these almost inconceivable concepts were, in fact, entirely possible. Yet even in those dreams that contained the highest degree of continual awareness, I noticed there was always a tendency for things to keep "popping up" on their own. Even now, twenty-some years later, I have never heard of anyone who claimed to have gained total conscious control of a dream environment. There seems to be some kind of force, or instinctive wisdom, behind the dream that allows only limited manipulation of the dreamscape.

The following is an example from my journals of a CNE that occurred spontaneously during sleep. Although I maintained a high degree of awareness and intentional action throughout the experience, the vast majority of the dream appeared without my having consciously created it. There was only one aspect over which I felt I had total control. That was my ability to consciously choose how I would respond to the situations that arose.

The Twilight Zone

Maggie and I are in our living room visiting with two old friends from Colorado, Vicki and Steve. As we step outside onto the lawn, I suddenly realize we are actually at the house we used to live in, which is a few miles away from our present home. Since our friends have never been to either house, they don't notice anything, but Maggie says, "That's funny, I'd forgotten we had come to the old house. I was thinking we were back at home." Her comment verifies what I've already begun to suspect; that we're in some kind of non-physical reality. I forcefully reply, "We DIDN'T go to the old house! We're in a parallel reality—a kind of Twilight Zone."

Maggie considers the possibility, but isn't completely convinced. Steve says nothing, but appears to be uncomfortable with the idea. Vicki looks at me as if I were insane and changes the subject. The four of us begin strolling up the street. As we reach an intersection at the top of a small hill, everyone suddenly realizes that what I said is true. Just beyond the stop sign, the dreamscape abruptly changes from a Florida summer afternoon to a snowy winter evening in the shopping district of a large city. We pause at the border. Maggie, Vicki, and Steve are all stunned to speechlessness.

I break the silence with a laugh and say, "Now do you believe me? Come on, let's explore!" The instant we step over the border, we all find ourselves dressed appropriately for winter. We see a bakery just ahead that still has its lights on. We press our noses against the cold glass, steaming up the display window that is filled with delicious smelling pastries. Further on, we come to a bus terminal. We decide to leave everything we are carrying here so as to be unencumbered. As we continue on our way, I realize that Steve is again assuming that this cold winter evening is the one and only "real world."

"This isn't real!" I shout at him excitedly, "it's a dream, and anything can happen!" As soon as the words are out I regret having said them, because I know I will wake up. For a second, everything flickers like lamps during a lightning storm. But I manage to regain my composure and the dream stabilizes again.

After exploring a little longer, we all agree that we should start back. We retrace our path to the bus terminal and are delighted to find our belongings still intact. Next we come to a busy intersection that we need to cross in order to get back to our own reality. We wait several minutes for the traffic light to change. Finally I decide it must be stuck and urge my friends to cross with me anyway. Vicki and Steve are reluctant and remain on that side, but Maggie comes with me. We dodge our way through the traffic to the far side and wave goodbye to our friends.

The last obstacle Maggie and I encounter on our way back is a dangerous railroad crossing. She crosses first and I lose sight of her. Then I step across the shiny silver tracks and suddenly have the sensation of slipping back into my physical body. I open my eyes and find myself lying awake in bed next to Maggie.

The entire experience was so incredibly vivid that I felt certain Maggie must have arrived in bed just moments before I awakened. Only after lying there for several minutes did I feel reacquainted with the laws of physical existence. Even then I couldn't resist asking Maggie if she'd had any unusual dreams. To my disappointment, she didn't remember any dreams at all.

This type of confusion, occurring at the fringes of a dream, is not uncommon. It constitutes what could be described as a sort of "psychic border dispute." The closer you are to the boundary between a dream and physical reality, the more difficult it is to determine precisely where the perimeters lie. You may encounter at these boundaries some of the most puzzling moments of your life. For instance, it is not unusual to think you have awakened when, in fact, you are still asleep. These False Awakenings, as they are called, are intensified by their typically high level of self-awareness and dreamscapes that are near perfect replicas of your physical environment. The experience may be frightening or even humorous, depending largely on your ability to adapt to the unfamiliar. Regardless of how they are experienced, False Awakenings raise some very challenging questions about the nature of reality, as illustrated by the following dream.

The Torn Scroll

The first dream is about Peter. It has a pleasant feeling as well as some suggestions concerning our conversation last night. I wake up during the night and write the dream down on my yellow legal pad along with a fairly detailed interpretation. As I lie down to go back to sleep, however, I begin to have doubts that I physically wrote it down. I think I might have only dreamed I did. Since I don't want to forget the dream, I go through the entire process again. Once more, I begin having doubts that I actually put it on paper. So the third time, I sit up in bed, look around my room and note the time on the digital clock. I even knock on my night table to make sure I'm awake. Then I write down the dream and interpretation one last time. Finally satisfied, I allow myself to go back to sleep in hopes of catching another dream.

In my second dream, there is a scroll of ancient teachings. A small surface tear on the face of the scroll prevents me from being able to decipher its meaning. I find a way to mend the tear and the teachings again become readable. They have something to do with the word "fulfillment." I awaken myself and record the dream. I know intuitively that the scrolls represent knowledge of the soul and that they were made incomprehensible by an emotional trauma. I write that the mending of the tear represents some recent soul searching and that once again the teachings will begin to make sense and bring fulfillment.

At this point, I suddenly opened my physical eyes for the first time since I'd gone to sleep. It was 8:00 a.m.. As I reached over to look at my notepad, I smacked my palm against my forehead and laughed. Except for the date and a brief predream entry, the pad was completely blank. This is all I could remember.

As this example shows, it's difficult to devise an infallible "reality check" even if it occurs to you to do one. Although the classic "pinch me" test may seem like a good idea, I can assure you that a dream pinch can feel every bit as real as a physical one. Another common test is to attempt to fly. But here again, there are complications. Even in a dream, you can only fly if you believe it's possible. The best tip I've learned for determining whether you are dreaming or awake is to find something to read and then read it over again. If the letters keep changing between readings, you are dreaming. If not, you can be pretty certain you are awake.

CNEs are powerful and intriguing experiences that transcend the boundaries of traditional religion and philosophy. Understandably, there is often a strong urge to contact others who have encountered these events. As I began to correspond and meet with dream explorers from around the world, I found many of the characteristics of CNEs that I had encountered being confirmed by others. The first thing I noticed was that CNEs are an object of intense fascination to everyone who has ever had one. They may even be too fascinating. People who have encountered them are often so enthralled by the experience itself that they tend to overlook the content. This is an unfortunate penchant, for some of my most valuable insights have come through the symbolism of CNEs as revealed by the Guided Interview approach.

Probably the most outstanding and frequently described characteristic of a CNE is the sensation of being fully empowered. At its best, this empowerment enables the dreamer to confront difficulties consciously and fearlessly and to implement creative solutions. Yet I discovered that this capability was also being used in ways that deeply concerned me. For instance, I encountered remarkably talented dreamers who were using their abilities to escape unpleasant confrontations by manipulating dream circumstances. While this might initially seem an enviable skill, it has about the same effectiveness as the little Dutch boy who poked his finger in one hole after another in hopes of holding up the crumbling dike. At best, it only postpones the inevitable.

Invariably, the same types of problems they escaped in the original dream start creeping into the newly created dreamscape. It's as if that Greater Wisdom grants us the ability to superficially manipulate our dreams, but continues to deliver the same unresolved issues up from the depths. Dreamers who persist in wrestling for complete mastery of their dreams may succumb to a habit of compulsive "dream-hopping." They don't dare remain too long in any one dreamscape because they learn that eventually the same kinds of situations will resurface. The irony of the situation is that the dreamer, while absorbed in honing his ability to create a variety of dreamscapes, fails to recognize his role in creating the waking situation his dreams are urging him to address.

For these reasons, I keep a watchful eye on what sometimes seems to be the propagation of a "lucidity cult" in contemporary dream literature. This viewpoint tends to perceive lucidity as the ultimate goal of dreamwork and look with disdain on "normal" dreams. Unfortunately, simply bringing a near-waking awareness into the dream state by no means guarantees any advancement toward enlightenment. In fact, in overemphasizing the importance of lucidity and intentional action in dreams, a source of deeper wisdom may be overlooked. After all, a fundamental function of dreams is to put the dreamer in touch with a greater realm of knowledge than is available to him consciously.

Whether or not you are able to maintain conscious awareness in your dreams, it is counterproductive to avoid unpleasant experiences. And your dreams won't let you get away with it for long anyway. That does not mean, however, that you are supposed to endlessly endure disturbing dreams. It simply means the disturbing dreams need to be confronted.

Earlier in the book I've described how the Guided Interview approach can be used to acknowledge previously unrecognized aspects of your larger Self. By giving your dream characters mottos, for example, you can begin to see situations from more than one isolated viewpoint. This broadened perspective helps to integrate the various aspects of your true being into one harmonious whole. Intentional or lucid dreams, then, are simply ways to facilitate this same integration within the dream itself. Instead of running away from a dream aggressor, for instance, you might consciously decide to try an alternative response. Stand your ground and confront your adversary face-to-face. Ask it what it wants of you. Use your lucidity to try out creative solutions.

Although the incorporation of intentional action into the dream state can open a vast realm of new possibilities, there are still certain limitations. For example, whether you are speaking of dying or dreaming, the phrase, "You can't take it with you" generally holds true. At least in terms of possessions. But there is something of great value you can smuggle across the border between waking and dreaming states: a credo. By "credo" I mean a synopsis of your highest ideals, condensed into a brief statement. It is similar to the mottos that are used in the worksheet, but broader in its scope. Whereas a motto is designed to express a particular viewpoint in a particular situation, a credo encompasses the principles by which you would live your entire life. Even when you are conscious in the dream state, you will not have the same capacity for rational thought you have in waking life. Therefore, it's helpful to bring your credo into the dream state. It can assist you in making decisions at critical points in your dreams by reminding you of your highest ideals.

You bring a credo into your dreams just like you would any other intention: by raising its priority in your waking life. Live by your credo during the day and it will carry over effortlessly into your dreams. Your credo is profoundly personal. No matter how you word it, no one else will ever completely understand what it means to you. And that's okay, because it has nothing to do with anyone else. Until now, I have kept my own credo to myself. Perhaps I thought it would be judged as corny or inane. I almost chose to exclude it from this book as well; probably for the same reasons. But a credo is worthless if you don't strive to live by it, and mine requires that I include it here:

"Always make the loving choice."

I chose this phrase because it reminds me that at every moment, in both my waking life and in my dreams, I am making choices. And I want each choice I make to reflect my highest ideals. What does "make the loving choice" ultimately mean? That's something I can't explain, as I only know what it means to me.

Proponents of intentional or lucid dreaming claim impressive benefits. These include increased creativity and problem-solving skills, the ability to break free of habitual patterns, improved health, acceleration of learning abilities, and an easier acceptance of physical mortality. But there is another benefit that may be the most valuable of all, though it is rarely mentioned. By developing our natural ability to direct our dreams intentionally, we can catch a rare glimpse of what lies beyond the sphere of our needs and desires.

I once took a cross country trip with my brother and his young son, Joshua. My brother, anticipating the needs of a two-year-old, had brought along a large box of toys and trinkets. It was not long before Josh began to clamor for a toy car. No sooner had I handed it to him than he began wailing for something else. That, too, I got for him. Invariably, I found that as soon as I would give him one toy, he would begin to cry for another. In order to hasten the inevitable, I gathered up every toy in the box and piled them onto Josh's lap faster than he could even ask for them. Soon, all I could see of my nephew was a Cheshire-cat grin peering out of an enormous mountain of toys. Then he gleefully battled his way out, knocking them every which way until his seat was again completely bare. Although he was toyless just as before, he was no longer dissatisfied. Something had changed and the rest of the trip was a delight.

Somewhere within each of us is that same little two-year-old, so preoccupied with our cravings that we lose touch with our natural state of joy. We can easily spend an entire lifetime attempting to appease our desires, only to discover that the satisfaction of desires is not the same as feeling satisfied. So why should we waste an entire physical lifetime finding that out when we can acquire the same experience through our dreams in a fraction of the time? Indulge yourself in your dreams. Ask yourself as you're falling asleep, "What do I really want?" Then, through your dreams, find out if you still want what you think you want once it's in your hands. For the sooner we discover that life is more than the satisfaction of desires, the sooner we can get on with the real business at hand: learning to love.

After several years of actively pursuing full awareness in my dreams, I noticed something interesting beginning to happen. The easier it became to maintain that state of awareness, the less important it seemed. The repeated satisfaction of my every whim in the dream state led me to the shocking realization that there was a limit to my desires. At a certain point I found myself having "reruns" simply because I did not know what to want anymore.

The next example is representative of this period when I first began to question, in a broader sense, the purpose and value of maintaining constant vigilance in my dreams. Our close friends, Russ and Julia, had invited Maggie and me to attend the birth of their second child. The call came one morning at 3:00 a.m.. Russ told us they were on their way to the birthing center. Maggie and I met them there and spent the next couple of hours waiting with them. Around 5:00 a.m., the midwife told us it looked like it would be several more hours. She suggested we all go back home for awhile. After returning home, I slept and had this dream:

Surrendered Lucidity at the Birthing Center

I'm in the birthing center, making a cup of tea in the kitchen. Maggie, Russ, Julia, and all her sisters are here as well. Julia has baked a fresh angel food cake and placed it on a table in the waiting room with a bowl of icing beside it. The cake looks perfect; it's moist and golden brown. I feel like I shouldn't disturb the cake, but don't see any harm in sampling the icing. I dip my finger in and try it. It tastes terrible and leaves a bitter aftertaste in my mouth.

Then I walk back into the birthing room to rejoin the others. Something about seeing them strikes me as curious. I say, "I just dreamed I was in here with all of you...," Then it occurs to me that I might still be dreaming and I add, "You know, I'm dreaming right now. I'm sure of it."

I decide to test it and walk outside. The others follow me out of curiosity, appearing to be somewhat concerned about my state of mind. A large truck is coming up the street. I step directly in front of it, holding my hand out in front of me. I'm confident it can't hurt me. It comes to an instantaneous stop about a foot away from my hand. Then it occurs to me that I should be able to pick it up. I grab the bumper with one hand and easily lift the front end of the truck. Once it's in the air, I give it a twist, and the entire truck falls over on its side. I decide the final test is whether or not I can fly. I take a few steps, hop Superman-style, and take off. I fly a few loops in joyous delight, then land and rejoin my friends.

They quickly get over their surprise at my demonstration and soon lose interest. We all go back inside the birthing center and chat in the kitchen as if nothing unusual had happened. There is a feeling of warm friendship and acceptance that I want to share, but feel distracted by the vigilance required to maintain my state of awareness. Finally I get tired of dividing my attention. I decide that whether I realize I'm dreaming or not, all I want is to be able to completely enjoy the company of my friends.

By this point, everyone is getting ready for an evening stroll. As we all jostle down the street, talking and laughing together, I deliberately stop maintaining my lucidity and feel it start to fade away. I'm thinking, "It doesn't matter—there's nothing more incredible than the joy I'm feeling right now...."

This dream was fascinating for several reasons. First of all, it was an extremely vivid CNE. Also, it was the first time I deliberately renounced lucidity in a dream. And just as significantly, I had strong and immediate associations with the imagery. More than once during the last few weeks of Julia's pregnancy, I had joked with her about the baby needing to "cook a little longer." So when I considered the "angel" food cake in the dream, I knew it represented the baby; the new little Earth Angel. Then I recalled the part about the cake turning out perfectly, but the icing leaving a bad taste in my mouth. It struck me that the dream might be foreshadowing a healthy baby, but unpleasantness surrounding the delivery. It turned out to be correct on both counts, as their healthy son was very nearly born in the car during their second trip to the birthing center.

The main lesson I learned from this dream, however, was that self-monitoring in dreams can sometimes get in the way of more important things. Obviously, my main concern when I had gone to sleep was the birth. The dream predictably addressed that concern, apparently even offering insights into its outcome. But the moment I became conscious within the dream, maintaining lucidity necessarily became my top priority. It began to steal the limelight away from the birth and everything else that was happening. But when it finally came down to choosing between maintaining lucidity and fully giving myself to the experience of love, I preferred the love.

A certain peripheral self-awareness is helpful, even necessary, during a dream. Without it we can over-identify with one role, perhaps allowing ourselves to believe we are nothing more than a helpless victim of circumstance. Yet over-attentiveness to the fact that we are dreaming can be equally limiting. The very attempt to maintain continual vigilance can be a distraction that interferes with our ability to comprehend and appreciate the point of the dream.

As an analogy, consider the dreamer as an actor. The dream is his current production and is obviously intended to have some kind of effect upon the audience. For the movie or play to be successful, the actor must maintain a balance between two extremes. If he totally loses himself in the role, then he may forget when the scene is over that he is more than just that one role. But if, on the other hand, he is continually reminding himself, "I am an actor, I am an actor...," then his acting will be transparent and the scene will lose its impact. So what he needs to do is keep the awareness that he is an actor tucked away in his back pocket, so to speak, while submerging himself in his role as fully as possible.

What I am advocating, then, is a state of relaxed awareness as opposed to one of diligent self-consciousness. Although the experience of total consciousness in the dream state still occurs spontaneously on occasion, I rarely strive for it anymore. It's like being granted the power to move mountains, only to learn that the Greater Wisdom has already placed them exactly where they belong. I now find that I generally prefer to relinquish control to the Greater

Wisdom and simply maintain my "back-pocket lucidity." Without getting in the way of my dream experience, it gives me the courage to confront any dream character, which has in turn eliminated any feelings of being victimized. It also enables me to intentionally carry my waking ideals into the dream state and act on them there. This has not only improved the quality of my dreams but of my waking life as well, since each affects the other.

The following dream exemplifies the kind of balance I strive for between dream consciousness and surrender to the Greater Wisdom:

Contacting The Elf-Spirits

I'm riding on horseback with about a dozen friends under a full moon. I suddenly realize I'm dreaming and pull up my horse to appreciate the beauty of the moment more fully. Then I let the awareness slip away. My friends notice I've stopped and come back to join me. We're looking for Elf-Spirits who were once physically embodied, but are now invisible. My friends consider me the "mystic" of the group, and expect me to lead them to the Elf-Spirits. I don't know where to look either, but happen to glance down and notice an imprint in the dirt. It's an Elf-Spirit symbol (which looks like an Egyptian Ankh). I scoop up the dirt without disturbing the imprint and turn, kneeling, toward the full moon.

As I do, its light begins to intensify. A spaceship, with an incredibly bright light beneath it, is flying toward us from the direction of the moon. The horses spook and my friends all scatter into the woods for protection from the blinding brilliance. I, too, am scared but again become lucid just long enough to remind myself that death is nothing to fear, then again let it go. I remain kneeling with my offering. The spaceship hovers briefly over my head, bathing me in intense white light, then flies away.

My friends begin to emerge from the woods and ask what happened. Again, I'm simultaneously aware of my dreaming and waking lives. As I stand there, I'm suddenly struck by the powerful realization that the way to reembody the Elf-Spirits in the physical world is through my writing.

Because dreams feed upon waking thoughts and actions, you are constantly influencing the content of your dreams whether you realize it or not. Intentional dreaming and CNEs are simply a matter of doing it consciously. As you become more aware *of* your dreams, you will naturally become more aware *within* them as well. Yet no matter how adept you become at intentionally influencing your dreams, you will be faced with the inescapable fact that the vast majority of your dream content will continue to come unbidden, for reasons of its own. So feel free to explore. You're not going to upset the balance of nature by experimenting within your dreams. The Greater Wisdom will make certain of that!

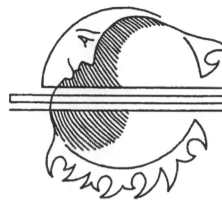

Chapter 11

Dreams that Foreshadow the Future

Of the many facets of dream study, one of the most perplexing and thought provoking is the frequent claim that dreams can depict future events. The list of questions that arises from this statement is endless. Are such claims blatant fraudulence? Are they a result of distorted memory or coincidence? If precognitive dreams do exist, does it follow that our lives are completely predestined? Or is it possible to prevent a precognitive dream from occurring? And if we *are* able to prevent it, then how can we claim the dream was a precognition?

In trying to present a straightforward, systematic approach to understanding dreams, I have risked oversimplifying them. They are, in fact, fascinating and complex phenomena that convey meaning on many levels simultaneously. Dreams are the crossroads of consciousness. People have ascribed them to the trickery of the devil or the wisdom of God, depending upon the prevailing culture, religious beliefs, and era. The consultation of dreams has been viewed as both blasphemous and sacred. Yet it is only our cultural perceptions that constantly change. The nature of dreams is unaffected by the whims of society and continues to serve its mysterious purpose just as it has always done.

As a dream educator, I am regularly approached by people who fear that terrible dreams they have had will prove to be prophetic. Lisa, whose dream appeared in Chapter 8, was an example of such an individual. My usual response to these kinds of concerns is to stress that such dreams are undoubtedly reflecting the emotional present, but not necessarily predicting the physical future. I encourage these people to work with their dreams and act on the insights they receive. To quote the old adage, "Take care of the present, and the future will take care of itself." Usually, as was the case with Lisa's dream, the message goes no further than the symbolic level.

There are times, though, when people come to me with tales of dreams that did appear to come true. Their stories range from the mundane to the outrageous. I have heard countless stories of people running into an old friend or receiving a phone call from them in a dream just hours before the event physically occurred. Many people have also shared very powerful dreams with me that seemed to fore-shadow births and deaths of loved ones.

Once, after I had appeared on a local television program, a woman called claiming to have had a powerful precognitive dream in the early 1960s. She told me she had been advised in a dream to buy up hundreds of acres of swampland near what was then the backwoods town of Kissimmee, Florida. The intensity of the dream motivated her to investigate the possibility of acting on it. Since she lacked the personal resources to purchase the land, she approached her relatives with the idea and was, understandably, flatly refused. According to her story, the swampland in question was selected a few years later as the site for Disney World.

I often find myself at a loss for words when told of such events. Since most of these kinds of reports are inadequately documented it would be easy to dismiss them as fabrications, distortions, or even hallucinations but for one thing: my own dream journals are riddled with equally unbelievable tales I know to be true.

Because it is so easy for dreams, memory, and imagination to braid themselves into a revised story line, I have learned to maintain a healthy sense of skepticism. The first thing I look for when evaluating an apparent instance of precognition is a written and dated account of the dream recorded before the foreseen event. Of course, that only eliminates unintentional revisions. It doesn't prevent deliberate fraud. Therefore, so that I can personally attest to the authenticity of the next two examples, I have used foreshadowing dreams from my own journals. I don't wish to give the impression that my dreams are unusually inclined toward precognition. On the contrary, I'm convinced that everyone has such dreams regularly. Yet my journals are well documented and unless dream records are meticulously kept, it is virtually impossible to verify connections between a foreshadowing dream and the ensuing physical event.

The following dream occurred at 4:30 a.m. on September 6, 1981, while I was living in South Miami, Florida. It concerned one of my oldest friends, Tom, who was living in Orlando, about two hundred miles away.

Problems With Tom's House

Tom is considering buying a rundown house to fix up, and has asked me to look it over with him. We approach the house from behind and view the property through a telescope atop a small mound about fifty yards away.

As I look through the telescope, I first see a horse running around the back yard. Then I see a young girl, who lives in the next house to the right, come over to ride the horse. She gallops all over the yard, tearing up the grass without any apparent concern about the damage she is doing. She even jumps the horse up onto the roof at a point where it slopes down low to the ground. She rides around up there, damaging the roof as well.

In a somewhat feeble attempt to console my friend, I turn to Tom and say, "Well, that will stop when you move in." Tom nods, but looks concerned. Both of us have serious doubts about whether it will be a very pleasant house to own.

After writing down the dream, I sketched out a map of the area. The drawing included the house Tom was considering buying with the horse in the back yard. The small mound where Tom and I had stood viewing the rear of the house was drawn on the lower left corner. The offending neighbor's house was drawn on the right. I also drew a quarry-like area behind both of the houses that I had not mentioned in the written account. I noted in the sketch that it had been covered with motorcycle tracks where kids had apparently been riding dirt bikes.

The dream was vivid and I recalled it effortlessly. I recorded it in my journal as had been my habit for many years and then thought no more about it. Three months later, on November 16, 1981, I received a letter from Tom. He wrote that he had been out looking at some real estate and had just run across a really good buy on a "Handyman Special." He said that although the house needed quite a bit of work, the basic structure seemed sound. He invited me to come up for the weekend and look it over with him.

Between my dream of Tom's house and the day I received his letter, I had recorded more than a hundred dreams in my journals. The September 6th entry remained forgotten among them. Even Tom's comment about the dilapidated condition of the house failed to jog my memory. Yet Tom was a close friend and it was his first move toward settling down after living in a modified schoolbus for nearly ten years, so I was interested to see what he was up to. On November 21, 1981, I arrived in Orlando. Tom and I caught up on each other's lives as he drove me to the property. I recall that we were laughing about something as he parked his car in front of the house and we stepped out. But my laughter stopped the instant I turned and saw the house.

An overwhelming feeling of déjà vu struck me speechless. The dream suddenly flooded back into me with such power that everything else seemed to fade away. I managed to say, "Wait!" as I attempted to open myself to the full memory. As the details came back to me, I recounted them to Tom. I told him we had approached the property from the rear in the dream, but that I was certain it was the same house. I told him about the horse in the back yard, the small mound we had stood upon and the quarry-like area covered with dirt bike trails.

Apprehensively, we walked around the side of the house. The first thing we saw in the back yard was a small horse tied to a post, grazing. Considering that it was a residential neighborhood, this was highly unusual. Then I noticed both the mound and a quarry-like area behind the property that was apparently being cleared for a new subdivision. It was covered with dirt bike trails. I recalled the problem with the neighbor in the dream and pointed out the corresponding house to Tom. It turned out that the horse did, indeed, belong to the daughter of that neighbor. When we realized he had no qualms about grazing his horse on someone else's property, we decided it would be wise to look for other possible infringements. What we discovered was that the neighbor had usurped a strip of land amounting to nearly a quarter of the lot that Tom was about to buy.

The property was a bargain though, and Tom later decided to buy it under the stipulation that the boundaries first be clearly delineated. After many unpleasant confrontations with the offending neighbor, Tom was eventually able to completely reclaim the property and remodel the house into a pleasant and attractive home for his family.

Dreams that appear to be precognitive at first glance often later seem to have been a likely result of subliminal perception. For instance, suppose you dream of a tire blowing out on your car. Then, the next day, it physically happens. The explanation could be that earlier you had semiconsciously noticed the glint of an embedded nail or that your tires had become dangerously worn. Even when such information is not consciously noted at the time, it may be subliminally perceived and later "re-presented" as a dream. It could be argued, then, that such dreams are not true precognitions. Yet it is often difficult, if not impossible, to determine with any certainty the extent to which subliminal perception may have influenced a foreshadowing dream.

It is conceivable, regarding my dream of Tom's house, that I might at some time have overheard my friend make a casual comment about looking at real estate. From my extensive knowledge of his personality and skills, I might even have been able to deduce that he would be attracted to a "Handyman Special." But the dream also revealed numerous details about the property and purchase considerations three full months before Tom had even seen the house himself. That seems to eliminate the subliminal perception explanation. Yet from a purely pragmatic point of view, it makes little difference whether a foreshadowing dream can be traced back to subliminal perceptions or not. The relevant question is, "How can I benefit from this insight?" Perhaps, instead of trying to categorize these dreams as either "psychic" or "explainable," our energy would be better spent in learning to understand the dream images and act wisely upon them.

The lesson I learned from the next example came at a high price.

Maggie and I had recently moved to the Central Florida area. The resettling period was difficult for both of us, but especially so for Maggie. While I had begun to make a few ties to the community through my work, Maggie was largely confined to home in caring for our two preschoolers. I was peripherally aware of her growing sense of isolation, but assumed it was her responsibility to seek a solution. Therefore, I did little to help. Then, around 7:00 a.m. on May 9, 1983, I had the following dream.

Couldn't Find The Hospital

Maggie, some friends, and I are in her green station wagon driving on Orange Street in north Orlando. Without warning, a young man with a gun steps out from the side of the road and forces Maggie to stop the car. He gets Maggie in the back seat and is holding her hostage. The guy seems real jittery and I'm afraid he might shoot her, so I jump around and make noises to draw his attention. He looks up. Then, thinking we're trying to trick him, he quickly spins around and shoots Maggie in the abdomen.

Time seems to stop. I can hardly believe what has happened, but feel a terrible sense of guilt knowing that I unintentionally caused him to pull the trigger. The next thing I know, the State Police have arrived and are taking the young criminal away. An ambulance comes for Maggie. I help the attendants lift her into it. As it drives off, I ask one of the troopers how to get to the hospital. There is some trouble in getting proper directions. I follow them as best I can, but am unable to find the hospital. I stop and ask several people how to get there, but they either don't know or give such rambling, confused answers as to be completely useless. It's not just people in the street I'm asking either, but service station attendants and professional people like nurses and lawyers. Still, no one can, or will, properly direct me.

I awakened shaking from the intensity of the dream, relieved to find Maggie sleeping safely beside me. Part of me felt I should tell her about the dream, but we had not been on very good terms for the past couple of weeks. I decided that telling her such a frightening dream was probably not the best way to reestablish communication. I rationalized my silence with the assumption that it would only further upset her. My biggest mistake, with the benefit of hindsight, was that I failed to fully acknowledge the urgency of the dream. It was not until thirty days later, on June 7, 1983, that I recognized its foreshadowing aspects.

On that day, I picked my son up from school in north Orlando. While driving home, we came upon the scene of an accident. Police cars and ambulances lined the road, but my view of the accident itself was blocked by a large truck. When the State Troopers motioned it past, I recognized the license plate on a smashed green station wagon as Maggie's. Although the sensations were similar, I cannot describe my response as a déjà vu. I think of déjà vu as an experience in which the present is confused with some dim, half-remembered past. In this instance, the memory of the dream snapped into my consciousness with crystal clarity. There was nothing dim or confusing about it. Instead, it seemed a strange merging of past, present, and future. I parked on the side of the road and walked toward the activity, searching my memory for details of the dream that might be of benefit.

The ambulance attendants were lifting Maggie into the back of the vehicle as I approached them and identified myself. They were unable to give me any idea about her condition. After they had driven off with her, I turned to the Troopers and recognized one of them as my neighbor. He told me that a young man, driving wildly, had swerved across the road at a blind curve and hit Maggie's car head-on while traveling at more than sixty miles per hour. He added that the young driver had appeared "extremely jittery and high strung, as if he were on drugs." Keeping in mind my dream, I asked where they had taken Maggie. He told me she would be taken to the Orlando Regional Medical Center on Orange Avenue. I was unfamiliar with that part of town. As my neighbor gave me directions, I remembered dreaming of Orange Street and the difficulty I'd had in getting clear directions. As a precaution, I wrote his directions down before dropping my son off with friends and leaving for the hospital.

When I arrived, a nurse at the admissions desk informed me that Maggie had not been brought there. As strange as it may sound, a profound calmness descended upon me. I felt I knew what was about to transpire and that Maggie would survive it. I walked over to the pay phone with a sense that I had already rehearsed the scene in my dream and needed only to play out my role as best I could. I called the State Police, informed them of the mixup and asked where the ambulance had taken my wife. The dispatcher replied that they do not keep records of where ambulances are sent. I then asked to speak to the Trooper who was my neighbor, and was told he had gone off duty. I tried a number of times, unsuccessfully, to reach him at home. After many more phone calls and misinformation, I finally located Maggie at a hospital several miles away on the other side of town.

I found her lying semiconscious in bed, badly cut and bruised. The doctor told me she had been lucky. The only serious injury was a fractured pelvis, which he said probably resulted from the steering wheel having been jammed into her abdomen.

Maggie lived as an invalid for the next month, confined to a wheelchair and requiring assistance for her most basic needs. She seemed to be living in a nether world, remembering nothing of the accident and often forgetting conversations from one day to the next. We spent nearly all our time together while she recuperated and I pondered frequently over the dream and all that had happened. I read and reread my dream account, always wondering whether I might have somehow been able to prevent the situation or if it was something Maggie was destined to go through.

The collision turned out to be a milestone in each of our lives for different reasons. Maggie, now fully recovered, often speaks of the incident as a rebirth. For me, it marked the beginning of an intensive search for a dependable way to identify precognitive dreams in time to act upon them. I began to focus my dream studies on finding ways to differentiate between precognitive dreams and "normal" ones. In addition to scrutinizing more than a hundred dreams in my journals that appeared to contain foreshadowing aspects, I consulted with other dream educators and researchers who shared my interest.

A few possibilities surfaced that seemed to deserve closer scrutiny. One red flag was the appearance of special recurrent symbols. For instance, I occasionally receive telephone calls in my dreams from people who are well known to me in waking life. On a hunch, I began to follow up these dreams by physically contacting the person who had called me in the dream. Nearly every person I contacted conceded that the telephone message I had received from them in my dream accurately reflected recent thoughts they had been having. Thus, telephone calls became the first of several "highlighting symbols" that I hoped would eventually enable me to identify psychic dreams. I also found telescopes, cameras, and similar devices appearing in certain precognitive dreams, including the earlier example of "Tom's House." Telescopes seemed a promising highlighting symbol, since their purpose is to focus upon distant events and bring them up close where they can be clearly seen. The problem was that the highlighting symbols did not appear in all the precognitive dreams studied and were therefore not reliable indicators.

I later postulated that precognitive dreams might be recognized by a higher level of vividness or intensity. Again this proved to be generally, but not dependably, true. While most precognitive dreams had a higher than average level of intensity, not all intense dreams turned out to be precognitive.

My hopes rose and fell with each new possibility I examined until, eventually, I was forced to question my basic premise. Are there really any differences between precognitive dreams and so-called normal ones? Or could it be that *all* dreams are *potentially* precognitive? The idea exploded in my mind with implications shooting off in every direction. If it were true, it would mean that all dreams could be described as probable futures: symbolic extrapolations based upon the dreamer's current attitudes and expectations. It also would imply that nothing is predestined, but that every probability has its own momentum that may or may not be enough to carry it forth into physical reality. Then, after awakening, we would either be reinforcing or countering the momentum of our dreams through our every action, thought and choice.

Some of the most intriguing (and most common) precognitions are not linked to major life crises, but instead involve unremarkable everyday events. When a dream's forewarning prevents the dreamer from boarding an ill-fated jetliner, the obvious question is, "How could the dream have known?" Yet when a dream presages being short-changed at the hardware store, the question is not only "how" but "why?" My best guess is that these types of puny prophecies are another of the various ways that dreams call attention to themselves. Whereas nightmares are a way of demanding the dreamer's conscious attention, small precognitions tend to intrigue a dreamer into looking more closely for meaning.

When first learning to attend to their dreams, many people have a tendency to take the images too literally. This becomes especially significant when considering dreams as potential precognitions. For example, while dreams of death are often disturbing, the vast majority of such dreams are addressing a symbolic death, such as the end of a long term relationship or a way of life. And in the same way, it is tempting to regard especially vivid dreams of loved ones as literal prophecies. But before you run off to announce impending disaster or good fortune, there are a couple of points you may want to consider.

Nearly all dreams, precognitive or otherwise, primarily relate to circumstances in the dreamer's own life. The characters in your dreams may very well be displaying behavior of which you, the dreamer, need to be made aware. A dream of your clutzy Uncle Filbert's careless accident, for example, may actually be a warning that you, yourself, have recently been behaving as carelessly as your clumsy uncle. Another possibility is that the dream may be bringing to light angry feelings toward Uncle Filbert that you have been harboring unconsciously.

Before assuming that the dream is literally about Uncle Filbert then, I suggest you first work with the dream along the lines of the Guided Interview Worksheet. This may illuminate feelings that were not immediately apparent and help you to decide whether it's wise to worry poor Uncle Filbert with your dream. Even when an event that was foreshadowed in your dream does physically occur, I still advise you to consider the dream as a symbolic reflection of your own situation as well. Dreams are often literal and symbolic at the same time.

Occasionally, I encounter individuals who report precognitive dreams of accidents or natural disasters that at first glance appear not to have involved the dreamers personally in any way. Two dream-worker colleagues, for instance, told me of having exceptionally vivid dreams of an explosive volcanic eruption just days before the May, 1980, volcanic eruption of Mount St. Helens. One of them lived in California and the other in the Washington, D.C., area. Neither knew anyone whose life was directly affected by the eruption.

More recently, on January 25, 1988, a group of dreamers gathered in Michigan with the intention of requesting a precognitive dream. They focused their predream thoughts on "the next immobilizing environmental situation." Three of the seven group members dreamed of mudslides in a forested mountain area. About three weeks later, Rio de Janeiro was declared a disaster area when 275 people died in devastating floods and mudslides. Again, none of the dreamers had any personal connections with the mudslide victims.

In another instance, a neighbor told me of awakening in a panic around 9:30 a.m. Saturday morning, May 14, 1988. Without think-ing, she turned to her husband and said, "My God—there's been a bus crash!" After fully awakening, she told him what she remembered of her dream. There had been a terrible accident; a bus load of children crashed into another vehicle—possibly a truck. She remembered no other details, just the horrible moment of the crash and the confusion and panic that followed. Shortly afterward, she and her husband were sitting at the breakfast table watching the morning news on televi-sion. A report came on that left her stunned. Around 7:30 a.m. that morning, a church bus full of schoolchildren was returning to Radcliff, Kentucky, from an outing. A drunken driver struck the bus with his pickup truck, causing the bus's gas tank to rupture. Smoke from the ensuing fire resulted in the deaths of twenty-seven of the sixty-seven occupants.

I leave it to you to decide if these dreams were somehow linked to the actual physical events, or if they were simply coincidences. More important to me is the fact that the dreams did occur, and that each had a profound effect upon the dreamer. Assuming for the moment that the dreams were true precognitions, why would an individual with no emotional investment dream of an event that took place thousands of miles away? Since none of the dreamers involved had any personal acquaintance with people who were affected by the disasters, it seems unlikely that the dreams were intended as warnings. This would be particularly true in the case of the bus crash, since the physical event occurred about two hours before the dream. If the dreams did not occur for the purpose of preventing the calamities, then perhaps the reasons for the dreams lie within the dreamers themselves.

When searching for reasons to explain these types of dreams, one approach is to begin by assuming the dream had a purpose and then work backward from that point. It is possible, in other words, that looking at the dream's effect on the dreamer's life might suggest a hypothesis as to why the dream occurred. In all the previous examples, the overwhelming common denominator was the dreamer's fascination with the striking similarities between their dream and the actual physical event that followed. The fact that their dreams appeared to literally come true caused them to reflect on the dream/event over and over again. Working backward, since the result of the experience was that the dreamer's attention was repeatedly redirected toward the dream, then perhaps there was something about the dream content that was important for the dreamer to acknowledge.

Comments made by some of the dreamers suggest evidence for such a possibility. One of the individuals whose dream mirrored the Mount St. Helens eruption, for example, told me his preoccupation with the unusual dream resulted in valuable new insights into some "volcanic" upheavals that were going on in his own life at the time. Similarly, while one of the members of the Michigan group was describing her dream of houses collapsing down muddy hillsides, she mentioned that in the dream she had been concerned about the stability of her own house. In both cases, there was the sense that the dreamer's personal situation was somehow intertwined with the precognitive images of the dream. Of course, as with any other dream, the dreamer's own feelings are the only way to confirm such possibilities.

When working with dreams there is an inescapable sense that complex meanings are implicit on many levels simultaneously. Perhaps on one level a precognitive dream is simply a literal, though usually slightly distorted, perception. At the same time, the foreseen event may be somehow symbolic of a current situation in the dreamer's waking life. And on yet another level the dream may be serving a spiritual purpose by affirming and reinforcing the dreamer's inner connection to All That Is.

While dreams apparently do foreshadow physical events with some regularity, they seem resistant to attempts at manipulating them. I was once contacted by a gentleman who claimed his dreams frequently provided him with valuable tips for winning at the horse races. He did have some evidence to support his claim, but when I questioned him more closely he admitted that sometimes the dreams would indicate the right horses in the right order, but on the wrong day. My own dreams appeared to play a similar joke on me while I was writing this chapter. I had been researching precognition when I was carried into the spirit of things one night by a pleasant, but not especially vivid, dream in which I won a small prize in the Lottery. The dream depicted a chart of numbers from 1 to 100. The only number clearly indicated was a 5 that was circled in red, but I recalled 6 and 2 as being peripherally suggested as well. In the dream, I played the number 5 and won, although the only thing I bought with my winnings was a small ice cream cone.

Normally I am not particularly attracted to lotteries, but when I awakened I couldn't resist the temptation to give my dream a try. Since there was no game in which only a single number could be played, I tried a few variations of 5, 6, and 2. The next day I stopped by the convenience store where I had purchased the tickets and learned that none of the numbers won. But when I stopped by the Post Office on my way home I found an unexpected rebate check in my mailbox made out for exactly five dollars!

My point is that the future is malleable and even if precognitions do exist, there are simply too many factors involved to be able to dependably recognize them in advance. Even if you feel certain that a dream is foreshadowing future events, you still have only the same choices you would have with any dream: 1) continue visualizing and giving energy to the dream as it appeared, 2) consider what beneficial changes might be made and then visualize and act upon those changes, or 3) ignore the dream and let everything come as a surprise.

As you explore your dreams, you will undoubtedly encounter

many perplexing coincidences. You may be able to explain most of these enigmatic links between your dreams and waking life as self-fulfilling prophecies. Others might be accounted for in terms of subliminal perception. But every now and then there will come a dream that leaves you groping for an answer and questioning your most deeply held beliefs. Don't drive yourself crazy trying to figure it all out. Learn to accept these events gracefully, for they are evidence of your personal connection to the Great Mystery. If it were necessary to fully understand the essence of a natural force before benefiting from it, we would still be without electricity or even fire.

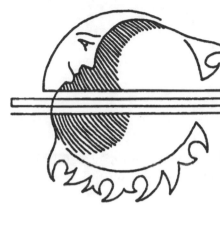

Chapter 12

The Theory
of
Thickening
Thought Forms

Or

How Dreams
Come True

When you study something long enough, the facts begin to form patterns, and those patterns tend to evolve into theories. This is what began to happen after I had spent several years examining the elusive borderline between physical and non-physical realities.

My investigation began in earnest in the spring of 1971 while participating in a psychic development group with some fellow students at Michigan State University. Using a biofeedback machine, we spent the first couple of weeks learning to enter deep states of relaxation at will. Then the leader of the group announced that our next project would be to "learn to view auras." She asked for a volunteer to sit in front of a black backdrop. The rest of us were instructed to go to a level of deep relaxation and just observe. After a few minutes, she asked each of us to describe what we saw. Nearly everyone stated that they noticed a sort of hazy glow around the subject's head and shoulders. Several group members described their observations in terms of colors, but not everyone agreed on which colors were present. What I saw looked more like an atmospheric disturbance—sort of like faintly tinted heat waves rising off a desert highway. The only hint of color I saw was a transparent touch of violets, pinks, and blues. It was not the first time I had seen this phenomenon that the group leader was calling an aura, but it was the first time I had ever really paid it any attention or given it a name.

As I walked home that evening, I found myself looking for, and finding, auras everywhere. Like a real life version of Van Gogh's

"Starry Night," even the sky itself danced with teeming, shimmering specks of light. I remained in fascination of auras for the next several days, occasionally being distracted during lectures at the university by the glow that surrounded the speakers. Gradually, I became aware of a related aural phenomenon. Again, it was nothing new, just a subtle perception I had never before considered worthy of acknowledging. If I had been asked to describe what it sounded like, I might have compared it to the pleasant, soothing symphony of crickets and frogs on a summer evening. Yet the musical droning was definitely not external. Instead of being muffled when I stopped up my ears, it became louder and more clear.

Once, while discussing spiritual development with an acquaintance in the medical field, I mentioned these perceptions. He suggested that the visual phenomena might be attributed to after-images or phosphenes (specks of light resulting from an excitation of the retina). As for the droning harmonies, he speculated that it might be a mild case of Tinnitus, or "ringing of the ears." Yet he was unable to explain why I only experienced these phenomena when I chose to tune into them. Despite my friend's scientific speculations, I was, and remain, certain that these experiences are not the result of any disease, but are instead perfectly natural perceptions that exist at the very edge of everyone's awareness. I'm convinced that the only reason most people are unaware of them is that no one has ever pointed them out. Thus, we have learned to ignore them and favor more "important" perceptions. I confess that for most of the twenty years or so since first becoming aware of these phenomena, I have ignored them myself. It's usually only when I'm alone in a quiet place or as I'm falling asleep that I pay attention to the shimmering, musical energy field. Although I can't deny its existence, I honestly don't know what to call it. My suspicion is that it is the basic fabric of the Universe that other cultures have called Prana, Chi, or Pure Energy.

Since the introduction of quantum physics, science now accepts the unlikely concept that light possesses characteristics of both waves and particles. Human thought also produces waves as nerve endings in the brain produce electrical impulses of varying frequencies. These brain waves can be traced and recorded by means of an electroencephalograph, or EEG machine. Suppose for a moment that thought, like light, exists in particle form as well as in waves. Theoretically, we would be constantly surrounded by a boundless sea of thought-particles similar in many ways to the shimmering, musical auras just described.

When a magnet is introduced into an energy field, it alters the pattern of that field. This is because the molecules of a magnet are not randomly distributed but are instead aligned, or focused in a single direction. Could it be possible that a clearly focused thought could have a similar effect on a field of thought-particles?

Consider a simplified explanation of how audio and video tapes are made. Recording tape, coated with easily magnetized particles, passes across a recording "head" that produces magnetic impulses. The magnetic impulses cause the random particles on the recording tape to realign themselves into a pattern that matches the magnetic impulses. Suddenly, the tape that was all static and noise a moment earlier is transformed into music and visual images.

Now imagine how a series of focused thoughts might act upon a field of easily affected thought-particles. Like magnetic impulses, strong, single-minded thoughts from your "head" could cause the thought-particles to realign themselves into patterns that match the original thoughts. Perhaps by repeatedly focusing our mind on the same types of thoughts, the field of thought-particles around us might gradually begin to realign itself in patterns similar to our projected thoughts.

To use a simpler analogy, when you repeatedly stroke a magnet across a nail, the nail will eventually become magnetized as well. Perhaps every time we have a thought, it is as if we are stroking a magnet one time across a nail. A single stroke will not magnetize the nail. A dozen strokes may begin to magnetize it to a small degree. But to fully magnetize the nail may take hundreds of strokes, or an extremely powerful magnet.

In the same way, it is unlikely that a single thought would have any significant realignment effect on the theoretical thought-particle energy field that surrounds us. The same thought repeated a dozen times, however, or one extremely powerful thought might begin to

have some minor effect. It may result in a low density thought-particle pattern that, while not physically perceivable, might be seen in an
alternate state of consciousness. It is even conceivable that what we
commonly call ideas, dreams, visions, or hallucinations consist of
these low density patterns.

Suppose that one of these low density thought-particle patterns
(I'll call it a "thin thought-form") was repeatedly focused upon by an
individual. With each recurrence of the thought, each "stroke of the
magnet" so to speak, the density of the thought-form would increase.
At a certain point the thin thought-form that was once merely an
idea would "thicken" into what might be called a personal belief. As
such, the individual holding that belief would be likely to act upon it.

Behavior reinforces attitudes more powerfully than mere thoughts.
Therefore, an individual's actions would undoubtedly strengthen a
thought-form even more than thoughts alone. In other words, ideas
lead to attitudes, attitudes lead to personal beliefs and personal beliefs
lead to physical behavior. And with each step, the original thin
thought-form thickens closer to becoming a personal reality.

Let's bring this down to earth for a minute with an example. In
the late 1800s, the most common form of transportation was a horse
and buggy. But then some guy who was tired of feeding and cleaning
up after his horse came up with the idea of a horseless carriage. That
idea, which could have come as a dream or other form of inspiration,
was at that point a thin thought-form. After having the original idea,
though, he probably thought about a horseless carriage every time he
cleaned out his stalls or paid a feed bill. And with each thought, the
thought-form thickened just a little more. Perhaps his next step was
to draw a sketch, which is often an idea's first step into physical reality. As he worked out potential problems on paper, he may have begun
to believe that the idea was possible. At that point, his idea would
have thickened into a personal belief. Once the idea became feasible
in his mind, he probably either started banging materials together or
hired someone to begin working on a prototype. In other words, his
idea thickened into a belief and his actions introduced that belief into
the physical world.

Of course, inventions are rarely the result of a single person's efforts. What happens when other people become involved? Just as brass sculptures in a park are polished by people who inadvertently rub them as they walk past, the density of a thought-form would increase each time someone happened to focus upon the idea. As the idea gains in popularity, its density as a thought-form increases correspondingly. Gradually it progresses along the spectrum from a dream to a personal belief to a personal reality. Then, as more and more people begin to accept the idea, it further thickens into a popular belief. If the pattern is reinforced by additional thoughts, it will eventually cross over into physical existence, perhaps as a manuscript or blueprint. Continued support for the idea would finally result in what we call a manifest physical reality, or an accepted fact.

The idea of a spectrum of increasingly dense thought-forms is not entirely unprecedented. Of the many wavelengths in the electromagnetic spectrum, for instance, only a narrow band are visible to human beings as light. We can see the colors of the rainbow, but not the longer wavelengths (such as infrared) and the shorter ones (such as ultraviolet). Certain insects can see these forms of light, however, as can humans who are equipped with delicate sensing devices. Sound also exists along a spectrum. Whales communicate at frequencies as low as 2 hertz and dolphins as high as 120,000 hertz. Yet since most humans cannot hear anything outside of the 20 to 20,000 hertz range, many of these elaborate ocean songs would not seem to us to even exist.

There is, of course, some variance in the range of vision and audibility between individuals as well as between species. Even one particular individual's ability to perceive extremes in sound and sight will vary depending upon his or her age, health, and state of mind. It seems likely, then, that the required density for a thought-form to be perceived also would vary among individuals. This might explain not only visions and hallucinations but paranormal sightings as well. Certain individuals might just have an innately wider range of perception. Perhaps their range was expanded through chemical influence or by a physical or emotional trauma. Under these conditions, it might be possible to perceive thought-forms that are slightly less dense than is normally required for physical perception.

In terms of the Thickening Thought-Form Theory, each of us acts as a broadcasting station with our every thought being sent out as a thin thought-form. Although these thin thought-forms are not perceivable in normal, waking consciousness, we may be able to perceive them while in the dream state or closely related states of consciousness. This simply means that in dreams, our own ideas as well as those of others can be seen and heard. Of this open market of thought-forms being broadcast, each of us might be attracted to certain thought patterns just as we have individual television preferences. As our dreaming attention gravitates toward these patterns we add to their density, both energizing and shaping them to some degree. This, in turn, brings those patterns slightly closer to becoming manifest physical realities.

A crucial point of this theory is that *density increases gradually*. Thin thought-forms are only observable in the dream state or states of similarly expanded awareness. Just as it takes many strokes of a magnet to magnetize a nail, a low density idea needs to be refocused a tremendous number of times before it acquires a high enough density to reach physical fruition. If we are longing for a heartfelt desire to manifest, this period of "thickening" might seem a needless and frustrating delay. Yet if every thought that occurred to us were suddenly to appear in our waking lives we would surely all be in trouble, for everyone has at least occasional nightmares and destructive fantasies. Therefore, the necessity of repeatedly reinforcing thought-forms over time would serve as a safety factor by allowing us ample opportunity to consider possible consequences and alternatives.

Evidence of an even greater safety factor is suggested in the perfect equilibrium of nature. This equilibrium or natural balance could be described as the Primordial Thought. Before humankind made its mark upon the earth, this Primordial Thought quietly kept the universe in balance. Even now, as we surround ourselves with the thought-forms that we have physically manifest, this Primordial Thought continues to drone on, overriding any extreme deviations with the power of its original pattern. All other thought-forms, constructive or destructive, exist only as long as they are continually refocused and energized. The moment we cease to vigilantly maintain them, they erode like sand sculptures back to the Primordial Thought.

So how, you might well ask, does the Theory of Thickening Thought-Forms apply to the practical use of dreams? Consider this:

1) From a limitless range of thought-forms, we each focus upon and energize a select group.

2) By concentrating on these thought-forms, we gradually thicken them into unique "life sculptures" that last as long as we continue to energize that particular pattern.

3) IT IS IN THE DREAM STATE THAT THESE THOUGHT-FORMS APPEAR FOR FINAL INSPECTION BEFORE BECOMING A MANIFEST PHYSICAL REALITY. This means that regular dreamwork will enable you to "preview" possible futures, so that you can energize those that you would like to see physically manifest and redesign the others.

The vividness of a particular dream directly coincides with its density as a thought-form. The more intense the dream, the denser the thought-form. And the denser the thought-form, the closer it is to physical manifestation *unless you replace it with an alternate pattern.* For according to the Theory of Thickening Thought-Forms, no event is destined to be. Up until the very moment an event physically occurs, it exists only as a thought-form that can yet be altered.

Dreams, then, are like the quality control department of our lives. They provide one last opportunity to make changes before thought-forms appear in our waking experience as physical realities. Simply by acknowledging your dreams, you will begin affecting changes in their content. Your awareness of your dreams makes you a conscious participant in the creation of both personal and collective realities. Dreamwork offers the incredible opportunity to preview and edit thought-forms before they reach sufficient density to pass into physical existence.

Two questions may arise at this point:

1) If, in my dream, I encounter thought-forms I would like to summon into my waking life, what can I do to speed things up?

Anytime you encounter desirable thought-forms in your dreams, by all means energize them! Relive the most emotionally satisfying parts. Let your thoughts frequently return to the dream images to "stroke the magnet against the nail," so to speak. If you have not already written the dream down, do so. Sketching, mapping out, or making magazine photo collages of your dream will reinforce the desired thought-form, increasing its density and hastening its development. You also might try writing out the essence of the dream as an affirmation.

Affirmations, repeated daily, are powerful means of increasing the density of a thought-form. To affirm something means to make it solid or declare it to be a fact. Classic affirmations such as, "Every day in every way, I'm getting better and better," are time tested means of intentionally influencing your life for the better. But condensing a favorite dream into an affirmation personalizes it and makes the affirmation more powerful.

For example, I once had a 37-year-old man in class who had recurrently dreamed of hiding from "wild Indians" since he was a child. Dreamwork revealed the forgotten memory that his strict parents had often disciplined him for "running around like a wild Indian." Soon afterward his parents divorced and he felt he had to be especially obedient and cooperative. It was then that the "wild Indian" within him became his enemy. After working with the dream, though it was many years later, he finally understood it was okay for him to let that "wild Indian" out to play now and then. One possible affirmation to solidify this understanding might be, "I am able to express my playful wildness safely and comfortably."

Perhaps the best way of all to thicken a favorite dream into waking life is to invent some way to act upon it physically, if only in some small, symbolic way. I recently had a wonderful dream, for instance, in which I was housesitting for a friend who was a pilot. The house was a virtual aviation museum, with experimental aircraft suspended from the cathedral ceiling and antique model airplanes displayed on all the walls. I chose to thicken this dream a few shades by attending an air show that featured experimental and antique aircraft.

2) If most of my dreams (and even most of the events in my waking life) are not what I want, how can I begin to make changes?

The first thing to understand is that no matter how much negativity and unpleasantness surrounds you, you don't have to "overcome" anything. You simply need to stop energizing the unwanted thoughts. Remember that all thought-forms are inherently short lived. Therefore, as you refocus your attention on desired patterns, the old ones will naturally erode back to the Primordial Thought of equilibrium of their own accord. If you fearfully avoid looking at unpleasant dreams or experiences, or judge yourself for having them, you are compounding your existing problems by continuing to give energy to thoughts of fear and judgment.

Instead, acknowledge your nightmares and then redream them. Imagine what you would do differently if you were in the same situation again. Then use the techniques already described to help thicken the density of the new thought-form. It's not enough to know what you don't like. You need new thought-forms to serve as a focus since you are always expending your creative energy on *something*, whether you are aware of it or not.

A friend from work came to me with a terribly disturbing dream her husband had told her that morning. In his dream, he had been in a hurry to go somewhere and had accidentally backed his car over their little granddaughter who was playing in the driveway. He awakened with an inconsolable feeling of sorrow and regret. The idea that he could have been so neglectful of her, even in a dream, was so upsetting to him that he cancelled his work appointments and spent the entire day playing with his granddaughter. This is a perfect example of making a conscious choice to divert energy from a possible future (and, more importantly, an emotional present) and using it to create a preferred future.

Naturally, it takes a certain amount of mental discipline to keep your thoughts focused on your preferred pattern. It also takes a certain amount of time, since all patterns develop gradually. But as you continue to focus on how you would like your life to be, instead of on what you don't like, you will begin to see evidence of the new patterns in your dreams. Use the feedback of your dreams to stay on course and make corrections as necessary. Before long, small improvements in your dreams will start to "thicken" into your waking life as well. Recognize these for what they are: proof that the new patterns are beginning to take root.

The Theory of Thickening Thought-Forms evolved from my observations of the interaction between various states of consciousness into a working model of physical creation. Does it really have any basis in fact? Is there really such a thing as a thought-particle field? All I know is that the more I act as if it were true, the more my life seems to verify it. So while the Thought-Form Theory may not yet have thickened into an accepted fact, I can subjectively attest that it makes a delightful personal reality.

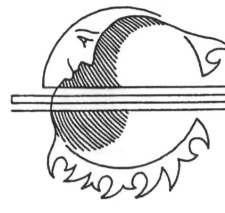

Chapter 13

E Pluribus Unum:

Out of Many, One

Our dreams are populated by characters of all persuasions. Most we recognize as people we know, or have known, in our waking lives. Some are famous personalities or fictional characters from television, literature, or the movies. Others are unfamiliar, but may have colorful or descriptive names. No matter how diverse their attitudes and personalities, they each share one common bond: every one of them is a co-inhabitant of our dream world.

There is an understandable inclination to view dream characters as literal equivalents of their waking counterparts. This is particularly evident when we dream of family members, close friends, or other people who are well known to us. The truth is that your dream characters usually appear for one of three reasons:

1) To bring to your attention some personality trait you and the dream character share in common that you have not been acknowledging.

2) To give you insights about the dream character's waking life counterpart (assuming it is someone you know) that might help you to better understand them.

3) To act as a stand-in for someone with whom you are closely involved in waking life.

A rule of thumb is that if you dream of a person who is unknown to you or not an active part of your life, they usually represent an aspect of yourself. However, it is necessary to view the character within the context of the dream to be certain. What is your relationship with them in the dream? Does their personality remind you of someone with whom you are similarly involved in waking life?

Even when you conclude that your dream is literally depicting a close family member or friend, it is important to recognize that they are not mirror image but adaptations or exaggerations of the people they represent. Still, seeing them through the eyes of our dreaming self may result in valid insights into their character.

Dreams that depict parent-child conflicts, for instance, often accurately mirror similar waking situations. On one level, the dream may be providing additional insights into the actual conflict. Yet dreams of generational conflict often continue even after the child has reached adulthood and the parents have ceased to be an active part of their life. The dreams may even continue after the parents have died. Does this mean the parents are reaching out from beyond the grave to harass their children? I don't think so. It seems more likely that the dream parent embodies the belief system once represented by the living parent and gradually internalized by the dreamer. Thus, the conflict is no longer between two people, but between two opposing characteristics within the dreamer's larger Self.

Most of us have a pretty strong opinion, either positive or negative, of who we are and what we are like. We readily accept evidence that supports this image. Yet thoughts and actions that do not conform to our self-image tend to be dismissed, often so automatically that they escape even the briefest acknowledgment. Dreams come to balance our self-perceptions, for it is a myth that any individual can be easily characterized by a few descriptive attributes. Each of us plays an infinite variety of roles during the course of a lifetime. Sometimes one rises to the forefront, sometimes another, depending upon the circumstances in which we find ourselves.

In dreams, our every conceivable characteristic is embodied in form. Each is given an appearance, demeanor, and even background perfectly suited to the role it was created to play. Some of these characters are more highly developed than others. Some have grown cruel and bitter from neglect. Yet you will find during dreamwork that even those you may have ignored for the better part of a lifetime are still remarkably responsive to even the smallest token of conscious attention. Simply by opening up enough to acknowledge them, you will come slightly closer to the point of emotional equilibrium I call the Comfort Zone.

Whether our dream characters are modeled after family members or appear to be complete strangers, they are undeniably members of our "inner family." Like biological descendants, the source of their being lies somewhere within us. Also like offspring, they each have their own personalities and follow their own paths. With some of them we feel a natural rapport. Others we may be less inclined to identify with, seeing them as either worse or better than we see ourselves. This is the root of all separatist thinking: believing that "we" cannot possibly be in any way similar to "them." Yet each time we deny any characteristic, judging it to be either undesirable or unobtainable, we are cutting ourselves off from our own wholeness.

Dreamwork is all about acknowledging these alienated characteristics: inviting them out of their hiding places and down off their pedestals. One by one, you will get to know them and empathize with their viewpoints as you begin to trust your dreams. In the process, you are likely to discover that the bad guys are not as despicable nor are the heroes as saintly as you may have assumed. At any rate, none of these "cast off characteristics" cease to exist simply because you have ignored them. Some remain latent possibilities of your own greatness. Others, having been exiled to the darkened corners of your consciousness, appear mutated or grown out of proportion when they visit your dreams. This banished group contains the characters no one likes to meet in their dreams. Predictably, the most common response to an encounter with these repugnant figures is to flee. Thus is born the Chase Dream, in which we strive to outwit or outrun our own shadows.

When I recorded the following series of recurrent Chase Dreams in my early journals, I was not analyzing my dreams at all. I was simply keeping as honest and accurate a record of them as possible. The gist of this early series involved my imprisonment and torture by cold, ruthless Nazi soldiers. It is important to understand that I had always prided myself on being self-sufficient, decisive, in charge of my own destiny. Therefore, it was extremely difficult even to acknowledge these dreams of being helplessly victimized. Only two things prevented me from shutting the dreams out of my consciousness altogether. One was the promise I had made to myself to be honest and candid in keeping my journals. The other was my faith in the value of dreams. And that faith was reaffirmed, for as I continued to record the dreams, I began to notice changes in their content.

In the earliest dreams, for instance, I was able to escape my oppressors only by awakening. Yet in a later dream I managed to get word to a nearby village. The courageous townspeople stormed the prison, overpowered the Nazis, and freed me from my shackles. I awakened ecstatic at the Nazis' first defeat, and hoped it would be the last of the dreams. It was not. For reasons I did not understand until much later, the dreams resumed after an extended reprieve. This time I found myself face-to-face with the Nazi commandant.

Escaped Nazi Death Camp

I'm locked in a stone fortress with no one around to help. I know the Nazi commandant is intent on torturing and killing me, so I have nothing to lose and everything to gain by resisting. For the first time since my imprisonment, I meet my enemy face-to-face. I curse him and defy his commands. He warns me that I will be sorry; that my death will be even slower and more painful than he had originally planned. But in accepting my death, I find I have lost all fear of it. I battle the commandant tooth and nail, wrestling him down and finally cracking his skull against the stone floor. After a stunned moment, I realize I have won my freedom. I run off into the open countryside, escaping the Nazi fortress....

This dream would have made an impressive ending to a Hollywood movie. I had confronted my greatest fear and conquered it in what I again hoped would prove to be the final battle. But again I was wrong. I had not yet learned the impermanence of victory: that defeated enemies never die but merely retreat into the nether worlds where they plan their resurgence.

I enjoyed another lengthy reprieve, unaware that on other levels of reality battle lines were again being drawn. What proved to be the final confrontation of this dream series took place outdoors on a river border between France and Germany. My previous efforts had apparently had some effect, for instead of Nazis, my enemies were now simple German soldiers. Their offenses were also less malevolent. Instead of being involved in torture and incarceration, they were now guilty only of preventing me from making an important telephone call. Yet since having lost my fear of the Germans, I vowed to never allow them to intimidate me again.

Formed Alliance With Germans

...My mission is to get past the German soldiers who are stationed on lookout platforms in the river, then locate and destroy their base of operation. I swim across the river, easily defeating several soldiers in the process. After some difficulty, I finally locate and penetrate the very heart of their headquarters. Here I encounter the top-ranking German officer. Unarmed and alone, we begin to wrestle. Hour after hour we struggle barehanded and evenly matched. More than once we back off in mutual exhaustion, then resume wrestling.

Finally, too tired to continue, we fall to our knees panting and sweating, leaning on each other for support. We both realize that neither of us will ever win. At that moment, a new sense of mutual respect emerges. I look at the German and say, "Listen, why don't we just forget all this and start working together?" He looks up, gives a tired smile, and offers his hand. We form an alliance right there on the spot. As I awaken, I know that this time the conflict is finally over.

It was not until years later that I began to fully understand the significance of the Nazi dreams. I had been in my early twenties when they first appeared. At that time, my self- image was that of a caring, easy-going new father and husband. True, my wife and closest friends had occasionally accused me of being stubbornly set in my ways. But what they might have seen as inflexibility, I called organization. I was completely blind to the fact that I was gradually becoming enslaved to the tyranny of perfectionism.

If I had taken the time to reflect on why Germany was so prominent in my dreams, a key symbol might have come to light. At the time of the dreams, I was working as a cabinetmaker, and my best tools were German made. Not surprisingly, I had come to associate Germany with precision, accuracy, and intolerance of error. Even when my dreams reflected this tendency back to me in the exaggerated form of Nazi ruthlessness, the symbolism eluded me. Yet it had taken a great deal of courage for me to even acknowledge the recurrent nightmares. Somehow that courage carried over into the dreams themselves and enabled me to confront the embodiment of my perfectionist aspect.

Even now, I am impressed by the wisdom of the final solution, though I can claim no credit for having consciously devised it. In making the German and me evenly matched in terms of both determination and stamina, the dream forced me to accept the truth. A love of precision and order is deeply rooted in my being. It should not, need not, and cannot be eliminated. But neither can I allow it to dominate over all other characteristics. There must be a balance between order and freedom; between precision and spontaneity.

Eventually, I learned to accept my precise German aspect, even to be grateful to it. For in recognizing that side of myself, I also discovered the heroic villager within me, the courageous lover of freedom and the tolerant, forgiving diplomat. Once I confronted the German, all the others could be allowed expression in my waking life as well.

It might seem self-evident that it would be much easier to accept our ideal aspects than to come to terms with our darker side. But this is not always the case. In fact, the chasms we create between our familiar and ideal aspects are often so wide as to appear unbridgeable. Fortunately our dreams not only make us aware of these disparities, but can provide us with opportunities to rectify them. A wonderful example of this was provided to me by Maggie. She described it as a "milestone" dream; one that proved to mark a major juncture in her life.

Reluctant To Admit Beautiful Girl (Maggie's dream)

I'm looking around in a real nice fabric or upholstery store. The girl in charge of the store is beautiful. She looks like Darryl Hanna, the actress. She's showing me a sofa she's upholstered. It's a pretty forest green with a raspberry-pink calico slip cover. The combination of colors is extremely attractive to me.

The beautiful girl is also a really nice person. She and I are talking and becoming friendly. The next thing I know, she is coming home with me. I'm not sure how it happened—maybe I invited her, or maybe she just offered to come over and help me by making some decorating suggestions. Everything is fine until we reach the apartment. The door is partway open, which means my husband, Will, is home. He hasn't seen us yet, and I realize I don't want him to see the beautiful girl. I'm afraid if he sees her, I'll be left out or ignored.

I'm hesitating at the threshold of the doorway, not wanting to invite the girl in but knowing it's too late. Just then Will sees us through the open doorway. He smiles and gestures for us to come in. I bolster up my courage and the girl and I enter. As I step inside, I let go of my insecurity and accept her presence. A profound sense of relief and relaxation sweeps away my feelings of intimidation. I'm suddenly free of the burden of feeling like I have to control the situation. The three of us all start talking together and it feels wonderful.

As I'm awakening, I understand that the reason I wanted to keep the beautiful girl away was because I've never believed there was a part of me that was like her. But in accepting her into my home, I realize I'm somehow accepting that she is a part of myself. I no longer feel the need to keep up a guard.

Recently, Maggie and I were reviewing the dream for its suitability as a book example. "This dream was definitely a turning point in my life," she commented. "By allowing this beautiful part of myself to come into my life, I was able to really relax for what felt like the first time in my life. The feeling stayed with me long after I awakened and to a large extent is with me even now, five years after having the dream. It has obviously had a lasting influence on my day-to-day life, because not only has my self-image improved, but I've even been put in charge of a real nice fabric and furniture store!"

In Maggie's "Beautiful Girl" dream, a new level of understanding was reached within the dream state itself. The same is true regarding the final dream of my Nazi series in which I first wrestled, then formed an alliance with, the German. Yet a quick glance through our dream journals would reveal that each of us had been dreaming about the same basic issues in various forms for some time. And between dreams, we not only wrote them down, but discussed the themes and images. In the process, both our dreams and our lives were constantly influenced in subtle but undeniable ways.

It is not simply that dreams improve the quality of our waking lives. Instead, it is the interaction between our dreaming and waking lives that improves the quality of them both. Just as both legs are necessary for graceful walking, both intellect and intuition are necessary for graceful living. This is the essence of dreamwork: to literally bring together the best of both worlds and form a united whole.

There is a simple mental exercise I call "Trading Places" that can sometimes help to facilitate this union. It can be done in any public place, but it is best to choose a location where people stay in one place for awhile. Airports, restaurants, classrooms, even traffic jams are all excellent settings. Find a spot where you can observe people discreetly and then select a subject. Your choice should be as random as possible—say, the third person you see. First, consider them from your normal viewpoint. Are they someone who would normally catch your attention? What feelings arise in you as you observe them? Are you at all attracted to them? Why, or why not? Next, imagine seeing the world through their eyes and experiencing it through their senses. Note how their reality differs from your own. What do you imagine is most important to them right at this moment? Is that ever important to you?

The purpose of this exercise is to expand the boundaries of your sense of self. In waking life, as in dreams, it is easiest to acknowledge people who seem most like ourselves. Those whom we view as the Others are often ignored or avoided until they force their way into our awareness. Exercises such as this, practiced regularly, carry over into the dream state where they lay the foundation for improved dialogue and understanding between all types of dream characters.

It is not necessary to agree with, or even like, your dream characters in order to hear them out. While you may not be able to condone their activities, it is worth your while to try to understand their perspective and motives and negotiate an agreement. Each of them has appeared to you for a reason. Yet only when you establish communication with them can you discover what that reason is. As long as you cling to the belief that the bad guys have to be eliminated, or that you can never be as courageous and wise as your dream heroes, then the deeper message of your dreams will elude you. For that message has to do with becoming whole. And wholeness results from a balanced integration of all your aspects.

It doesn't take long for the benefits of reclaiming these dissociated parts of ourselves to become apparent. One of the first things many people notice is a higher level of energy in their waking life. Since each of our dream characters is comprised of a portion of our inner force, it is not surprising that the integration of a previously disowned character often results in higher vitality. Increased interaction with your dream characters is likely to result in more satisfying relationships in your waking life as well. There is a great deal more exchange between the two realms than is generally acknowledged. Every step taken in the dream state leaves a faint corresponding footprint on solid earth.

Basic truths that you discover in dreams are also valid in waking life. Habitually acknowledging and honestly communicating with your co-inhabitants in the realm of dreams is equally effective when applied to citizens of the physical world. Each member of any race, religion, or culture represents the concerns of a certain element of planetary consciousness just as each of our dream characters reflects an aspect of our larger Self. The ability to see someone else's position from their own viewpoint— even when it is completely foreign to our usual perspective—is essential to wholeness, both personal and planetary.

In other words, the qualities of communication and integration needed to unite our planet are the same qualities that develop naturally as you learn to work with your dreams. It's unrealistic, of course, to expect the multitude of political, religious, and socio-economic factions in the world to suddenly merge together as you begin to acknowledge and understand your dreams. But as your own life moves toward the heart of the Comfort Zone, you simultaneously give the whole world a little push in the same direction. Consider this final example:

Each A Part Of The Other

I'm attending a conference, and find myself part of a group of twenty or thirty men and women. We're standing outside on a large, well-manicured lawn. We've all come here for the same purpose (possibly as representatives from our home areas), but we are all strangers to each other. We're milling about in a cluster, trying to reach a consensus as to where we should go as a group. Nearly everyone seems to have their own strongly held opinion about it. This makes everyone a bit defensive, and therefore a bit offensive as well.

I'm feeling increasingly uncomfortable, and fervently wish everyone would just stop bickering. I'm looking from one face to the next, watching each of them heatedly debate the validity of their position when I suddenly become aware that I am dreaming.

As that happens I say, "Wait a minute! This is all a dream… and every one of you is an aspect of me!" They all stop talking and look at me. Then after a long silence, they begin to look thoughtfully around at each other. Finally one man says, "He's right, it's true…and all of you are aspects of me!"

Within moments, all feelings of friction among the group melt away as we realize we are all a part of each other and that our needs are equally important. We run, skip, and leap joyfully across the lawn toward a little downtown café area that seems as good a destination as any. It's a delightful, childlike feeling. I'm laughing and running along behind the group saying, "… and even though you're all aspects of me, I give you the freedom to live however you choose!" But they already know that and pay no attention to my chatter, which doesn't bother me in the least.

Then I awakened, filled with joy.

Dreams provide an infinite variety of nighttime education and entertainment. They provide insights into waking situations, enable us to rehearse our responses and play out our fantasies. They show us ourselves as we are and as we might be. Remembered or not, they affect our mood and inspire us to take action. They remind us of forgotten values and make us aware of denied feelings. They put us in touch with the tender longing and fulfillment of romance and the bold courage of confrontation. They are the foundation of our conscience and the pinnacle of our hopes. They provide friends when we're lonely and solitude when we're not. They warn us when we're heading toward danger and guide us, if we're willing, back toward the Comfort Zone. They are a laboratory for experiments in consciousness and a fountain of creativity. In dreams we speak with animals, breathe underwater, and fly through the heavens. And for all this, what do we have to pay? We have to pay attention.

May you pay attention, and reap the rewards.

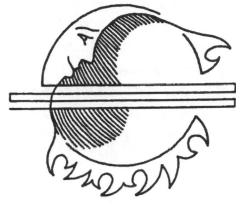

Appendix

The Guided Interview Worksheet

1) Recount the dream in the present tense, condensing the main elements into outline form:

Setting (Describe the location, time of day, season, point in history, weather, and mood.)

Characters (List the main characters or groups, whether they are human, animal, vegetable, or mineral.)

Event (Essentially, what is happening in the dream?)

Response (How do I respond to the main event? If I am not a participant in the dream, what is the response of the main character?)

Conclusion (What is the last thing I remember happening in the dream just before awakening?)

2) At the conclusion of the dream, I experienced feelings that I would plot on an emotional spectrum as:

horror fear frustration neutrality satisfaction happiness elation

|———————————————◆———————————————|

(Warning)   (Evaluation)   (Guidance)

3) On a scale of 1-10, I would rate the vividness/intensity of this dream as:

|———————————————◆———————————————|

0   1   2   3   4   5   6   7   8   9   10

(green)   (ripening)   (ripe)

4) In about 5 words, write a title that reflects the essence of your dream (refer to the Event in the SCERC outline).

Title: _____

5) Was there anything in the dream I was avoiding? If so, what was it and why was it important that I avoid it?

6) In this dream, the choice is:

Conformity vs. Individuality	Decisiveness vs. Acquiescence
Abundance vs. Need	Honesty vs. Deception
Freedom vs. Restriction	Desires vs. Loyalties
Separation vs. Reunion	Power vs. Impotence
Privacy vs. Exposure	Death vs. Rebirth
Vulnerability vs. Toughness	Confrontation vs. Avoidance
Imbalance vs. Equilibrium	Commitment vs. Desertion

Or: _____vs. _____

7) List the most outstanding images that appeared in the dream, along with a brief statement defining and describing each.

8) First, list the parties or groups involved in the main event. Next, write a short "motto" for each that represents the basic viewpoint of that character or group.

	Participants		Mottos
a)	_____	=	_____
b)	_____	=	_____
c)	_____	=	_____

9) Draw a simple sketch, or describe a "mental snapshot" of the most emotionally highly-charged scene in the dream.

10) Mentally project yourself into the scene you just drew. After the words, "I feel...," write at least three words that describe your state of emotion.

"I feel...":

11) In what kinds of WAKING situations have I had feelings similar to those just described in item #10?

12) What was most strongly on my mind before going to sleep? Or, what is the primary concern in my life at this time and what specific obstacles are in my path?

13) If I were to have this same dream again tonight, what (if anything) would I do differently to create a more satisfying outcome?
   a) ("Redreaming") Alter the sketch you made in response to item #9, incorporating any changes you would like to make.
   b) ("Paradreaming") If the conclusion of your dream was completely satisfying, consider what you would have liked to have happen next had you not awakened when you did.

14) How can I translate these dream improvements into waking terms I can act upon TODAY to similarly improve my physical situation?